MACHINE EMBROIDERY:

Ideas and Techniques

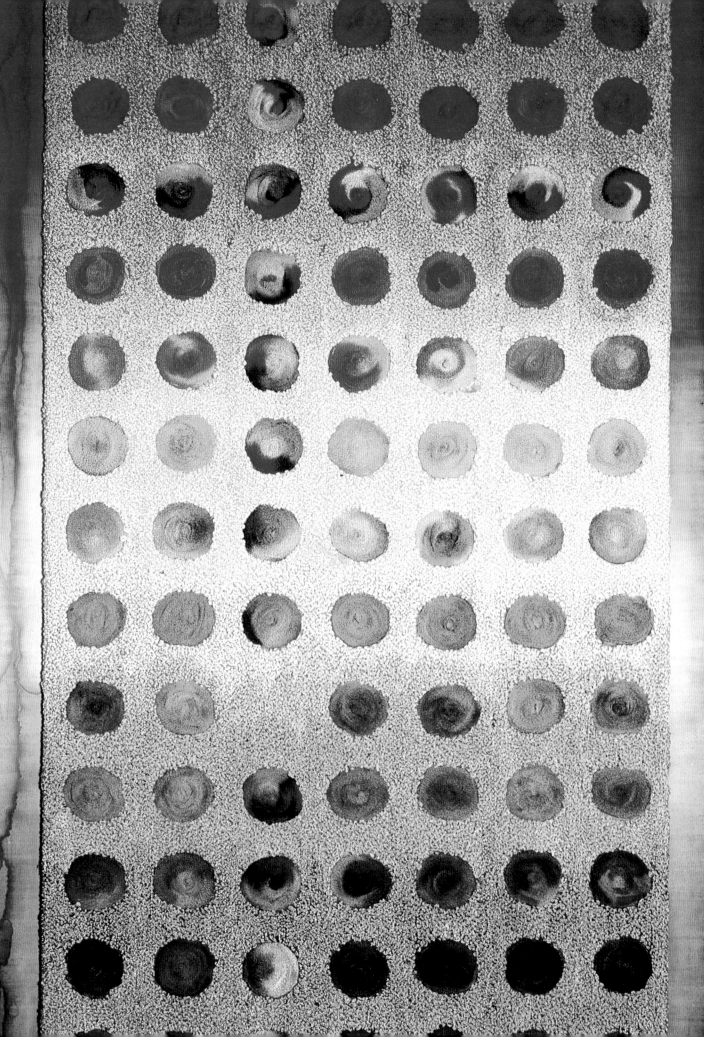

MACHINE EMBROIDERY:

Ideas and Techniques

PAMELA WATTS

B. T. Batsford Limited, London

JD950796
£15.95

Stock-take 2003

© Pamela Watts 1992
First published 1992

Typeset by Servis Filmsetting Ltd, Manchester
and printed in Hong Kong

For the publisher
B.T. Batsford Limited
4 Fitzhardinge Street
London W1H 0AH

A catalogue record for this book is available
from the British Library

ISBN 0 7134 6644 8

Jacket illustration
*Massed short lengths of silk thread applied to a background
with Bondaweb, covering it completely. These are further
secured with lines of narrow free satin stitch using a rayon
thread.*

Frontispiece
*Circles of very dense free running stitch worked on tights,
using white thread. After stitching, each circle was painted
before being applied to a textured, painted and stitched
background. The panel is framed on to a dyed and painted
fabric (Frances Manz).*

CONTENTS

ACKNOWLEDGEMENTS

My thanks to Rita Walsh, to my colleagues and to all the City and Guilds students at The Woking and Chertsey Adult Education Institute for their support and friendship over the years. I would like to express my admiration for the machine embroiderers in my last two City and Guilds groups at Woking and to thank them for allowing me to use their work to illustrate this book.

I am grateful to Valerie Campbell-Harding for her endless help, advice and encouragement and for taking some of the colour photographs.

I would like to thank everyone at Chipperfield Colour for developing and printing the black and white photographs.

My very special thanks go to David Partridge for his good humour, patience and care in photographing the embroidery for me.

Pamela Watts
Kings Langley 1991

The embroidery, drawings and diagrams are the work
of the author unless otherwise stated.

INTRODUCTION

LEARNING a new skill is very satisfying. The process also needs to be fun, with regular measures of success along the way. The aim of this book is to inspire you with enthusiasm and, above all, confidence in your own ability to machine embroider.

The majority of people learn about embroidery through hand techniques, whether at school or in later years. Then suddenly it seems that exhibitions,

Three quilted silk cushions.
Left: *A design of roses quilted with a twin needle and finished with a decorative stitched piping cord.*
Centre: *Log-cabin patchwork quilted with a repeat pattern of roses and finished with a machine-wrapped cord and a group of three tassels at each corner.*
Right: *Italian quilting on painted fabric with bands of free running stitch, using two threads in the needle. The cushion is finished with a frill, edged with the same band of stitching.*

books and magazines are featuring machine embroidery with ever-growing emphasis. Perhaps you have been shown a piece of work which you admire, or have seen a demonstration. You may have been introduced to machine embroidery during a class or just decided to try it out at home on your own machine.

The most common first reaction is that it has an unpredictable, even alarming, quality which is very different from the somewhat precise nature of hand embroidery. It can seem, at times, that your machine is an alien, just waiting to mystify you. You will come to realize that it is actually a wonderful, strong and precise machine which is capable of producing subtle and rich patterns and textures. These are not intended to mimic hand techniques: they are in no way 'automatic', but techniques in their own right.

This is a book essentially about what to do, and what to make, with your first attempts. Every success you have will give you the confidence to develop your skills even further. You will learn more about your machine and how different effects are achieved, and will develop a relaxed and familiar way of stitching on fabric to produce the exact effect you want every time. Predictable, yes, but always exciting.

Every time I sit at the machine, I learn something new. Perhaps the best way to use textured metallic threads, how to make machine-wrapped tassels or that the back of the work is sometimes far more exciting than the front! I hope that more experienced machine embroiderers will take a starting point from some of the ideas and techniques described and develop them still further.

The first chapters take the beginner through everything necessary to start embroidering, and the techniques of free stitching, appliqué and quilting. The last two chapters are devoted to what to make, from simple to more adventurous projects. You may have heard of cable stitch, whip stitch, and the need to alter your lower tension, but the vast majority of items described here use only two stitches: free running stitch and free zigzag stitch.

From these humble beginnings, you will discover that machine embroidery has infinite possibilities for anyone who owns an electric sewing machine.

1
STARTING TO EMBROIDER

YOUR MACHINE

It is quite wrong to assume that only the most expensive, latest model is capable of machine embroidery. If you have an electric swing-needle machine of virtually any vintage or make, you should be able to work through all the techniques described in this book. The only requirement is that your machine is in perfect working order: clean, oiled and warm!

Read the 'Maintenance' section in your manual and take time to clean and oil your machine as suggested. If you suspect that your machine has a fault, however simple, do have it professionally serviced. Machine embroidery seems to generate far more fluff than ordinary sewing, so make a habit of regularly brushing the race and removing any small pieces of loose thread.

Lastly, keep your machine in a warm room. The cupboard under the stairs is not a good place and a cold machine will seem very sluggish and ill-tempered.

FABRICS

Technically speaking, it is possible to machine on any fabric. However, for the moment, choose firm, closely woven fabrics such as calico, cotton or old sheeting for your first efforts. Avoid those fabrics which are very thin, very thick or, worst of all, stretchy. Patterned fabrics can suggest ideas as to where to stitch. You can follow lines, fill in areas, add emphasis to a flower by stitching round and round it, stitch curved lines on stripes, or straight lines on circles.

Fabric paints and crayons are now widely available in art and craft shops, and simple printing on your own plain fabric can be an excellent starting point. Buy two or three pots of paint in your favourite colours. The only other equipment you will need is an ordinary paint brush, a few pieces of old sponge and a plate.

Put two or three blobs of different coloured paint on the plate, swirling lightly together with the brush. Do not mix them too much. Dab a piece of sponge into the paint and touch on to the fabric. A simple

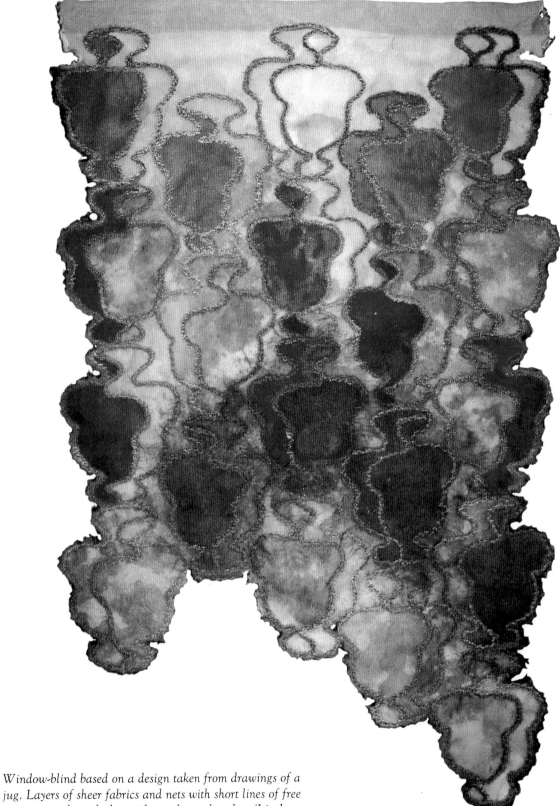

Window-blind based on a design taken from drawings of a jug. Layers of sheer fabrics and nets with short lines of free running stitch worked at right angles to the edges (Linda Cook).

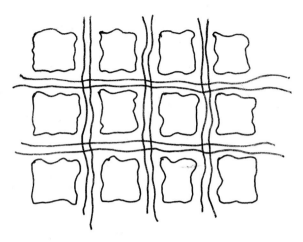

Emphasize flowers on a patterned fabric by adding lines of stitching around them on the background.

grid pattern of squares, blobs or circles is all that is required at this stage – a full-blown artistic design can come later!

The paint will give you an idea of where to start stitching, either on top of and around the shapes or, perhaps, filling in the spaces between them. You may decide, having worked some embroidery, to paint again on top of the stitching. The sequence is never-ending, but it will certainly produce more exciting results than a few hesitant lines of stitching on plain white fabric. After a while, you will want to try stitching on other types of fabric. It is amazing how the nature of the fabric alters the appearance of the stitching. Try working on felt, velvet, satin or textured fabrics such as dupion or furnishing fabrics.

Several layers of sheer fabric can give inspiration for stitching. Cut a number of simple shapes in different colours of organza, organdie or nets. Place these on a backing fabric, overlapping them, so that

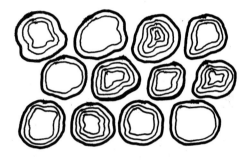

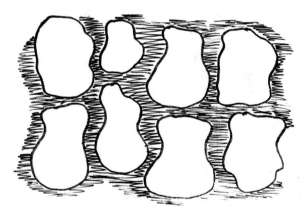

Simple patterns indicating areas of fabric printing with added stitching.

'new' colours and shapes result. Cover the whole area with a layer of sheer fabric to hold the pieces in place while you add the embroidery.

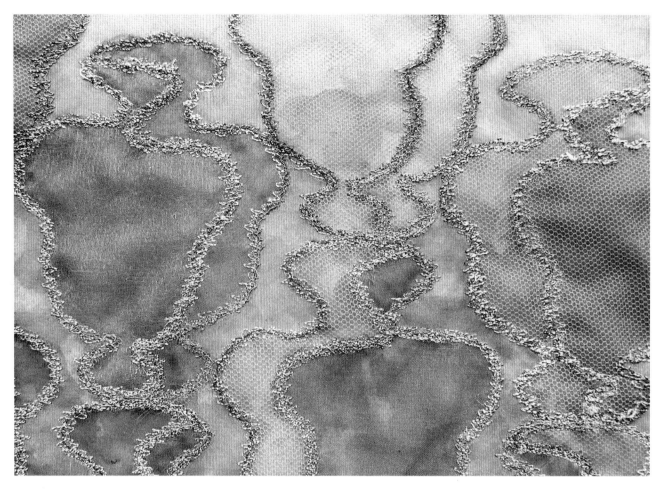

ABOVE:

Detail of window-blind, based on drawings of a jug. Layers of sheer fabrics and nets secured with short lines of free running stitch worked at right angles to the edges (Linda Cook).

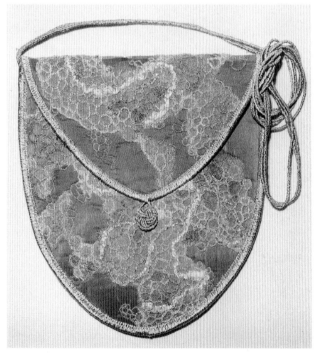

LEFT:

Free running stitch worked on chiffon and nets, applied to silk fabric with added stitching. A satin-stitched edge and machine-wrapped cords complete the bag (Celia Litchfield-Dunn).

STABILIZERS

When you see a sewing machine, or machine embroidery, being demonstrated, it is often not noticed that the fabric used is either very stiff or that two layers of fabric are being used together. This helps to eliminate the problem of the fabric puckering under the density of the stitching.

Try putting felt under your fabric or use one of the tear-away paper products made specifically to stabilize the embroidery (see page 92). Alternatively, you can use one of the iron-on interfacings usually sold for dressmaking, but these do tend to alter the feel and drape of the fabric, so bear this in mind.

You can use this extra stiffness to great advantage when working embroidery for a belt or bag, whereas on bed linen or a cushion, it would be disastrous. Get to know the various products by trying them out, and decide which is the most suitable for any particular project.

THREADS

Most beginners to machine embroidery come with a selection of threads acquired for the purposes of dressmaking and household sewing. Although these can obviously be used for embroidery, they do not give the attractive results produced by threads made specifically for machine embroidery. These are now more widely available, so do ask your local craft

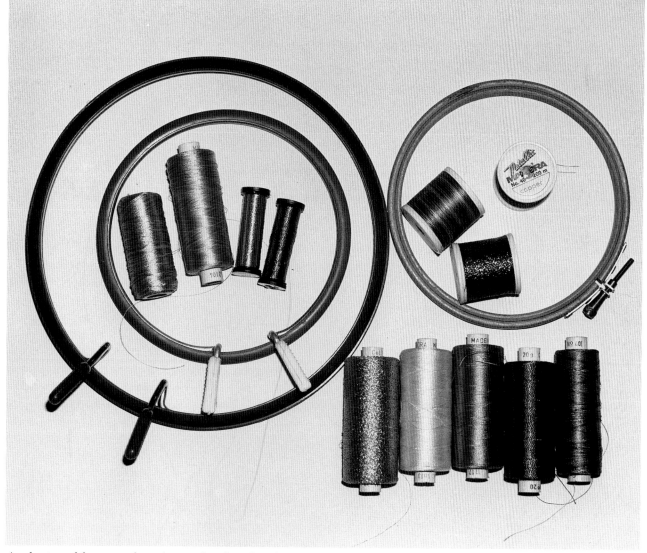

A selection of frames and machine-embroidery threads.

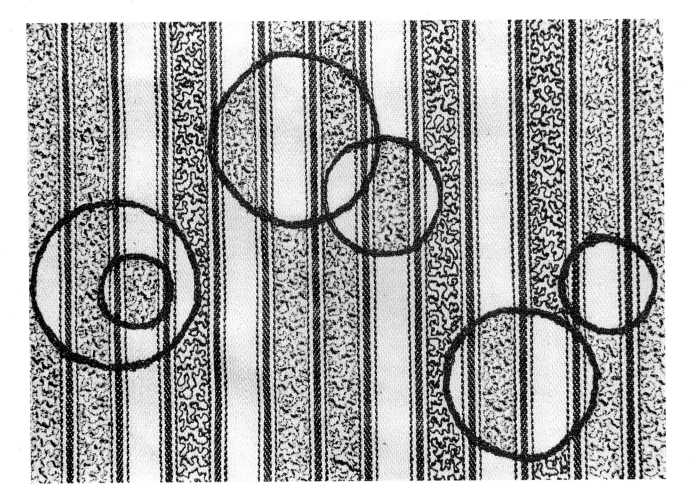

These circles were worked in several lines of free running stitch. The background fabric is pillow ticking with some stripes filled in with vermicelli stitch.

shop, embroidery friends or look in the advertisements in embroidery magazines to find your nearest stockist (see also the list of suppliers on page 95). Many suppliers offer excellent mail-order services, and the purchase of a shade card makes it very easy to order by post.

Surely there is not an embroiderer alive who is not inspired by the shaded, variegated and metallic threads available, and these can make even the simplest embroidery look wonderful. Fine rayon threads have a wonderful sheen and come in a very wide colour range. Buy the largest-size reel you can: the thousand-metre reel is much more economical than the smaller reels. Keep your threads in a covered container, as light (particularly sunlight) makes the thread brittle and likely to break.

METALLIC THREADS

Metallic threads are remarkably easy to use on the top of the machine, but many experienced machine embroiderers find them a problem. There are two simple rules:

1 *Reduce the top tension*
The thicker or more textured the thread, the looser the tension should be. On a machine with a top tension range of 0–10 (where 5 is normal) use a tension of between 2 and 3 for the thin, smooth threads, and down to 1 for the textured threads. Never machine with the top tension set at 0 as this can cause other problems. If your machine has a + and − (plus and minus) system, investigate the extent of the range and set your tension to correspond with the number system.

Altering the top tension of your machine does not harm it in any way, and you will always be able to return to the normal setting for ordinary sewing.

ABOVE:

Detail of embroidered pillow case and duvet cover. The printed heart motif is outlined in free running stitch, with added lines of satin stitch, using a variegated thread.

RIGHT:

Patterned gold fabric applied to black silk and heavily embroidered with free running stitch using a gold metallic thread. The top of the bag has a border of black silk pieces applied to the gold fabric, also embroidered with gold thread (Annette Monks).

2   *Use a larger-size needle*

For thin metallic threads, use a size 90 needle, but for the textured threads you must use a size 100 or even 110 (which is often sold as a 'jeans' needle). Use a new needle to begin with and replace it much more frequently than when using ordinary threads. The larger-size needles should prevent the 'shredding' of the thread which can happen just above the needle. It is also sensible to run the machine a little more slowly when using the textured metallic threads.

FRAMES

A small ring or tambour frame is essential for machine embroidery. A wooden frame with a tightening screw can be used for small areas of work, such as individual motifs, and does keep the fabric very taut. The disadvantage is that the work has to be removed from the machine to move the frame on for another part of the design.

Metal spring ring frames are also available for machine embroidery. They are thin enough to pass under the darning foot and even under the ordinary presser foot (wooden frames are usually too thick to allow this), and there are certain times when it is a great advantage to be able to use a ring frame in conjunction with a presser foot. Another benefit is that they can be moved along to another section of the design without removing the work from the machine. This is essential when embroidering a border pattern on sheets or towels, for example.

Do buy a good-quality metal ring frame, which should have grooves on the inside of the outer plastic ring. This helps considerably in gripping the fabric. Unlike wooden frames, metal spring frames do not seem to last a lifetime. The spring of the inner ring becomes weaker after continual use, so the purchase of a new one could be a wise investment from time to time.

NEEDLES

Use a new needle when starting to embroider. A size 90 needle is suitable for most fabrics and threads. Make sure it is fitted with the flat side of the shank to the rear and as high as possible into the needle socket. Change the needle frequently, as a blunt needle is one cause of skipped or missed stitches. Keep a supply of larger needles (100s and 110s) too, particularly if you intend to use metallic threads. If you experience problems with the thread shredding or fraying, then try using a larger-size needle.

FREE RUNNING STITCH

You may have heard machine embroidery described as 'drawing with the needle'. This is true, but many people are as nervous of drawing as they are of machine embroidery. The following method of starting machine embroidery has been devised to get over both of the above-mentioned hurdles. It really can be very easy.

1   Frame a piece of calico, preferably in a metal ring frame.
2   Thread your machine with a favourite colour, using a different colour on the bobbin. Use a synthetic or rayon thread if possible.
3   Lower or cover the feed dog. Refer to your manual for instructions on how to do this (probably given under *Darning*).
4   Replace the presser foot with a darning foot.

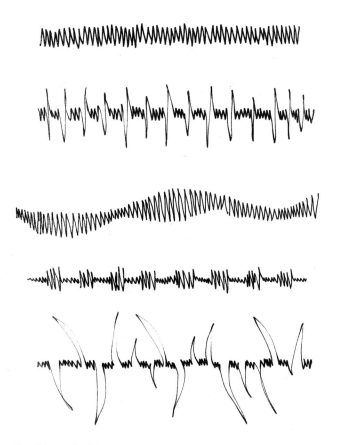

Confidence-building exercises for free running stitch.

A sampler of free-running-stitch exercises on painted fabrics.

5 Set the stitch-width and stitch-length controls to 0, and reduce the top tension to number 3 or the equivalent.

6 Place the framed fabric under the needle, with the fabric resting on the bed of the machine.

7 Turn the fly wheel towards you by hand so that the needle dips into the fabric, goes back up to its highest point and just starts to come down again. This brings the bobbin thread through to the surface, preventing it from becoming tangled underneath.

8 Lower the presser-foot lever. This engages the top-tension system.

This may seem to be a long list of instructions but it will soon become second nature. You are now ready to embroider. Forget, for the moment, any idea of 'drawing' with the needle. With your arms resting comfortably on the machine bed or worktable, start the machine running and move the frame away from and towards you, making short lines of stitching. This rocking movement of the frame, back and forth, is very relaxing and predictable.

Try varying the speed of the machine and moving the frame more quickly and then more slowly. When you stop stitching, get into the habit of leaving the needle down in the fabric. This prevents accidentally jerking the frame which can bend the needle.

These little solid bands of stitching are a very reassuring way of starting machine embroidery. If you 'miss' a bit, and the fabric shows, just go back and add the extra lines of stitching. This has much more structure and purpose than meandering around with haphazard lines of stitching, which is, incidentally, very difficult to do when you are feeling tense.

The secret is that while you are sewing these bands you are learning the feel and control of your machine. When you want to be more adventurous, breaking out into swirls and curves, you will find you have the ability and, above all, the confidence to work them.

If you do not have a darning foot for your machine, or it is so bulky and awkward as to prevent you seeing clearly where you are stitching, then you can work free running stitch without any presser foot in place. Many embroiderers work like this. Proceed exactly as already desribed, but ensure that you keep your hands on the edges of the frame, as the needle will now be unprotected.

Equally, if you only have a thick wooden-ring frame, try working without the darning foot; otherwise you will have to remove the darning foot every time you put the frame under the needle or remove it. Choose whichever combination suits you best.

Practise the rocking method of stitching until you feel completely happy with it. Try a variegated or shaded thread, and work bands in different colours, blending one row into another. The stitch diagrams on page 16 should give you some ideas, and you will invent many more of your own.

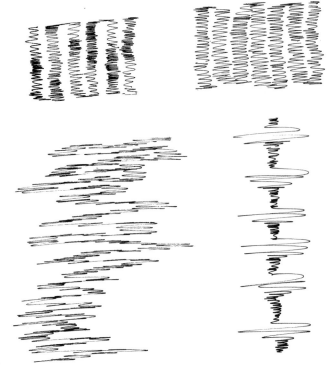

Suggestions for free zigzag stitching.

STARTING AND FINISHING THREADS

Make a habit of holding the top and bobbin threads to one side when starting to stitch. A few stitches on the spot will secure the threads and, when convenient, snip these off with a pair of sharp scissors. Finish off the threads in the same way by stitching on the spot.

When embroidering on something which will require frequent washing, such as bed linen, however, it is sensible to take all ends of thread to the back of the work, tying them off securely.

FREE ZIGZAG STITCH

Set your machine for swing-needle or satin stitch, choosing a wide stitch setting. Everything else remains the same as for free running stitch, but your needle will now move from side to side. If you are using a darning foot, turn the flywheel by hand to check that the width of the setting is within the width of the opening on the darning foot. Machine in short lines, up and down, so that the rows encroach on each other. Move the frame slowly for denser areas of stitching or more quickly for an open zigzag effect. Change to a narrower stitch width to add a further variation.

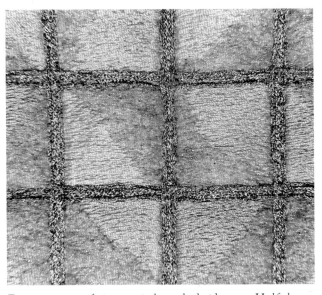

Dense squares of zigzag stitch worked sideways. Half the square is worked with a textured metallic thread, contrasting with a plain rayon thread.

Instead of moving the frame away from and towards you, try moving it from side to side. This will look completely different, with the stitches overlapping and building into a rich texture. This is the time to try one of the crinkly metallic threads which look so inviting. They are very easy to use for sideways zigzag, and areas of different colours can be blended into each other. This is perhaps the best and quickest way of completely covering the surface of the fabric with stitching. Contrast the texture of the metallic thread with areas of stitching using an ordinary rayon thread. Work through the stitch patterns suggested and, again, you will find your own favourites and special combinations.

Many of these simple patterns for free running stitch and free zigzag stitch have been used to embroider items illustrated in later chapters.

Remember that, as well as using satin stitch as a free-embroidery technique, it also has great potential for decorative effects used in the conventional way. Use the presser foot recommended for satin stitch (do not forget to raise the feed dog) and place the fabric in a metal ring frame.

Try working several lines of straight satin stitch

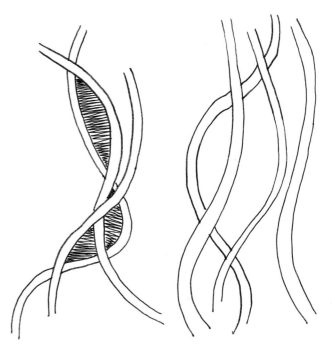

Curved lines of satin stitch to be worked with the presser foot on and the teeth or feed dog up. The shaded areas could be filled with short lines of free running stitch.

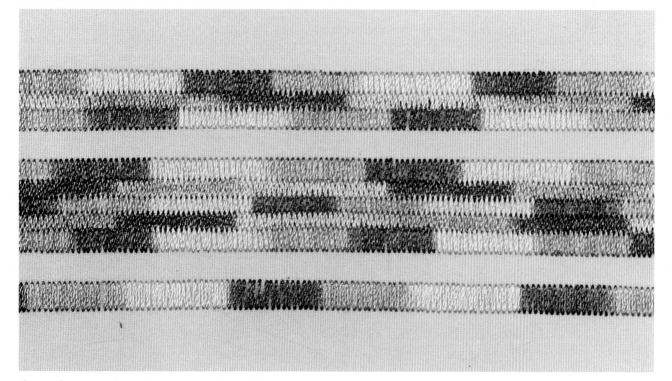

Rows of satin stitch worked close together with a narrow band of satin stitch covering the join.

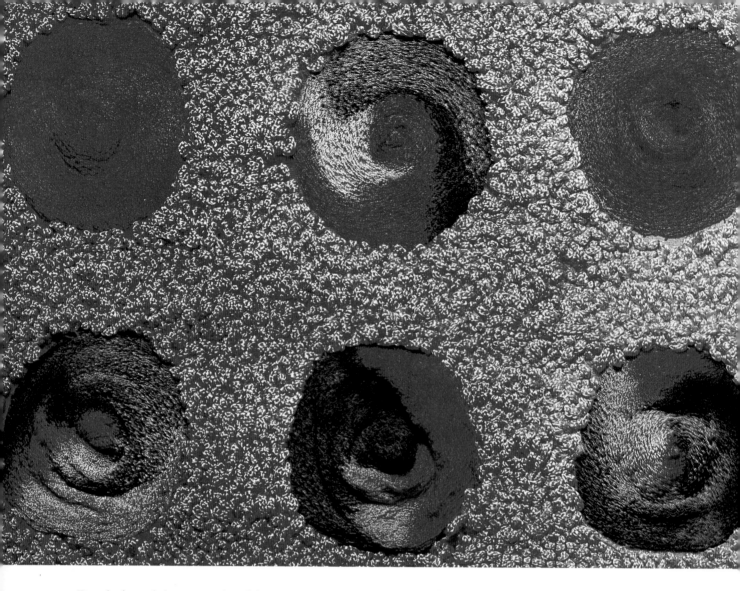

Detail of panel showing circles of free running stitch worked on tights. The density of the stitching produces the folded, sculpted effect which is raised in the centre of each circle (Frances Manz).

close together. This will look much more impressive than just a single line, with the appearance of a satin ribbon, especially if you use a shaded thread. It is difficult to stitch so that the edges of the lines just touch, so when you have worked two or three lines as accurately as you can, machine a narrow line of satin stitch over the join. This will look much nicer, turning a problem into a positive advantage. You will also be able to stitch in overlapping curving lines, made very much easier by the fact that you are holding the frame to control the movement of the fabric. The use of the frame also removes any tendency for the fabric to pucker.

TENSIONS

Assuming that your tensions are correct for ordinary sewing, at some stage in learning machine embroidery it will occur to you that your tensions are 'all wrong'. This is judged by the standards of dressmaking perhaps, but embroidery is a completely different skill. You will probably see specks of the lower colour, especially at the turning point of two lines of stitching. Regard this as a bonus – it can be a positive part of the design and colour effect. It happens when you move the frame slowly with the machine running fairly fast.

Try to make this happen on purpose. What you are doing is a variation of free running stitch called whip stitch, where loops of the lower bobbin thread completely encase the top thread. It is a most attractive stitch – heavier and more textured than free running stitch. You can encourage this effect by increasing or tightening the top tension as well as moving the frame more slowly.

The flower shapes shown in the diagram on page 30, worked on tights in free running stitch. After cutting away the surrounding area of tights, the petals curl and twist as shown.

If, of course, you do not want the colour on the bobbin to show at all, then it would be wise to use the same colour on the spool and bobbin.

As a general rule for free running stitch, the only tension alteration you need to make is to reduce the top tension. I would recommend doing this when you are using rayon threads, especially if you have had problems with the top thread breaking whilst stitching.

COLOUR EFFECTS

As mentioned in the previous section, it is likely that you will achieve a speckled effect when using different colours on the bobbin and spool. This need not be a dramatic colour difference. Imagine an area of green stitching with a shaded green thread showing through from the bobbin, adding life and vitality to your embroidery; or a metallic thread on top with rayon underneath matching the colour of the fabric. It is often a mistake to use colours which contrast too strongly with the fabric. Make the most of the sheen of rayon threads by using the same colour of fabric and thread, or just a shade or two lighter or darker.

As a machine embroiderer, it is essential to get used to the idea of changing your top and bobbin threads as often as the design demands. This is somewhat alien to the principle of dressmaking or household sewing, where it is normal to use the same colour thread throughout. It really only takes a

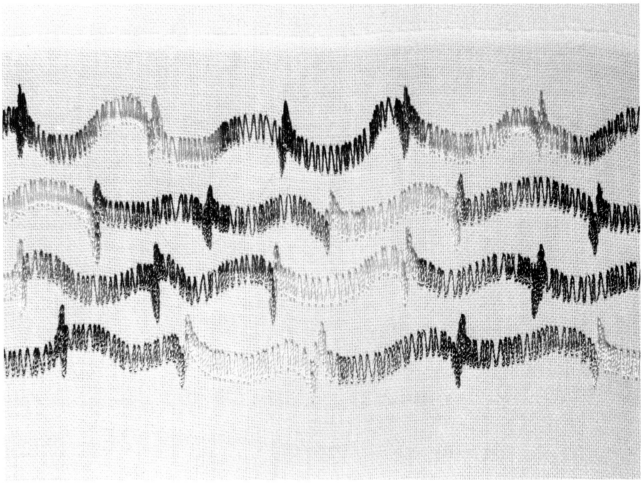

Zigzag stitch worked freely with some areas worked sideways.

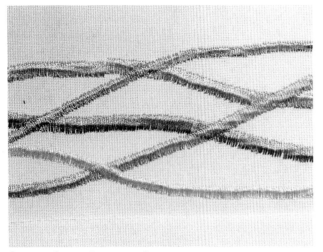

Crossing lines of satin stitch.

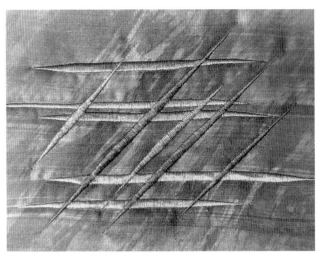

Tapering lines of satin stitch worked on a painted background fabric.

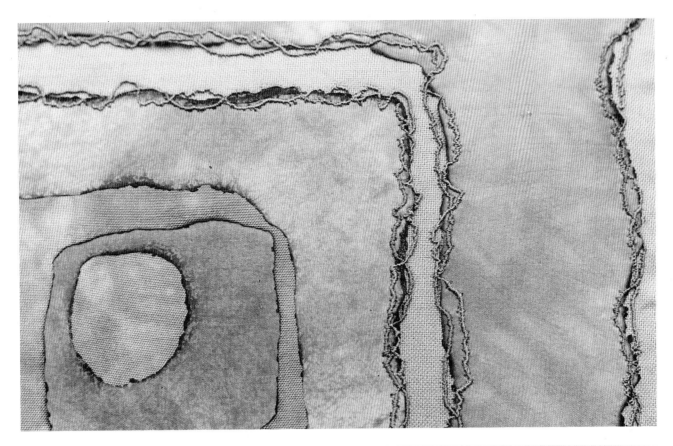

ABOVE:
Meandering lines of very narrow free satin stitch used to secure the edges of appliqué.

RIGHT:
Small bag worked with completely solid squares of free running stitch (Annette Monks).

minute to change the thread and it is always worth the effort.

Make sure you have plenty of bobbins. You will always need more than you have, especially as it is a golden rule never to wind one colour of thread on top of another. Keep your old, empty cotton reels and wind unwanted bobbin threads on to these for use another time.

USING TWO THREADS IN THE NEEDLE

Every time you embroider, you are faced with choosing a colour. Sometimes this is obvious, but, when faced with indecision, try using two colours together in the needle. This gives either a lively or a subtle effect, and adds greater density to the stitching. It is particularly useful when using variegated or shaded threads, which can appear as definite blocks of each colour in turn. With two strands together in the needle, a mixture of all the colours results.

If your machine has two spool pins, place a reel on each, threading the machine with the two threads together as usual. When you reach the tension disc, put the two threads one at each side of the disc, continue threading as normal and feed through the needle together. A size 90 needle will be correct for two fine rayon threads, but use a size 100 for thicker threads, and reduce the top tension.

If your machine does not have two spool pins, check to see if your bobbins will fit on the spool pin. If so, wind a bobbin, and place this on the spool pin with the reel of thread on top. This is also useful if you have only one reel of the variegated or shaded thread you wish to use.

If neither of these methods is possible with your machine, then a little ingenuity is required. Fill a very small jar with *Blu-tack* or a similar re-usable adhesive, covering the top of the jar with a circle of thin card with a hole in the middle. Stick a short length of thin dowelling firmly through the hole, placing the jar behind your machine. This becomes your second spool pin.

ABOVE RIGHT:
Ways in which template shapes could be transferred to build into border patterns and motifs.

Simple landscapes showing some of the stitch patterns suggested.

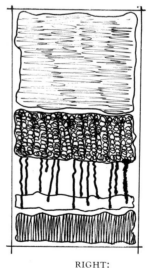

RIGHT:
Applied squares and rectangles of shot-silk fabric, secured with free running stitch. The four sides of each shape were then frayed back to the stitching lines.

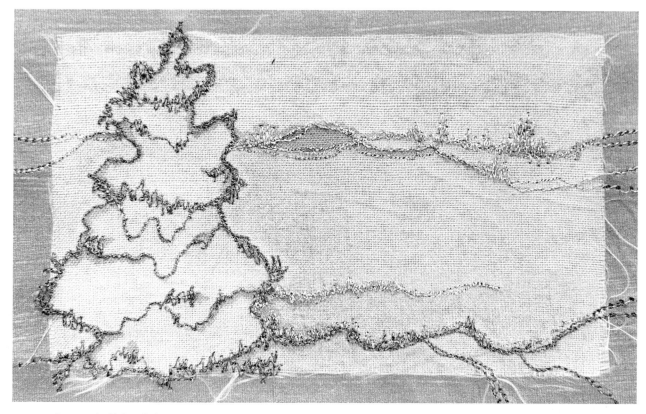

ABOVE: *Scrap of silk bonded to painted paper with free running stitch in rayon and metallic threads.*

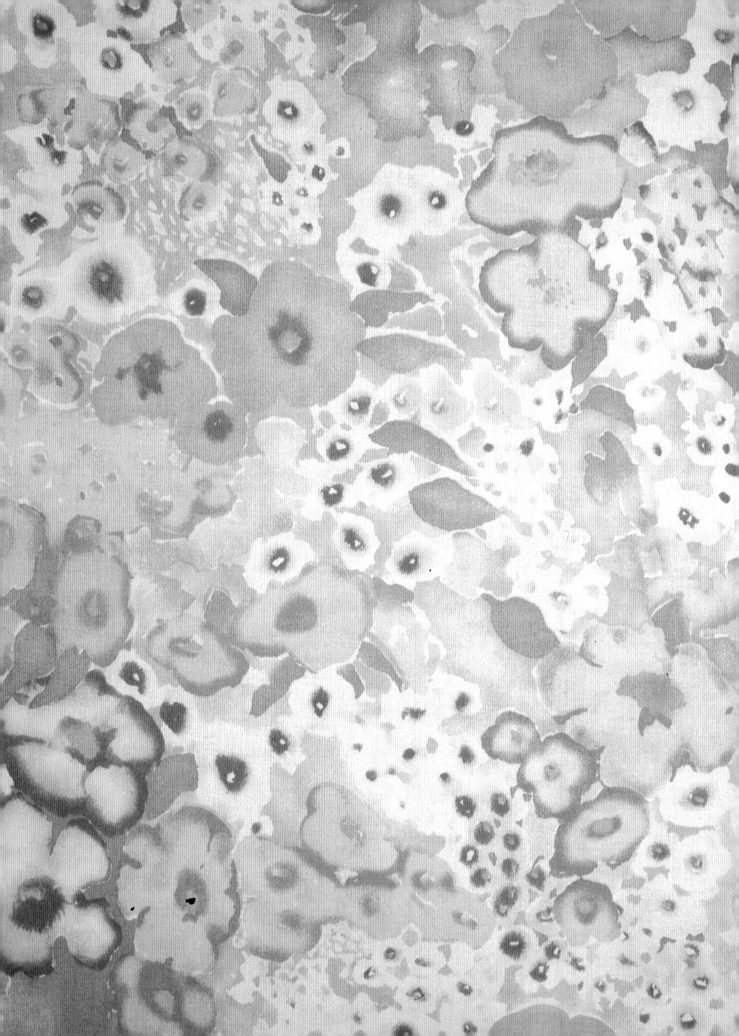

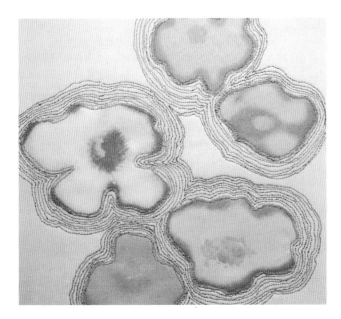

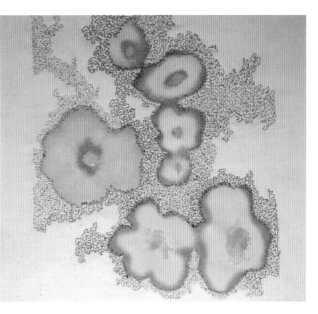

The main photograph (left) is of a patterned curtain fabric. The two embroideries above show flower motifs cut from the fabric and applied to a plain white cotton. Free running stitch is added in lines following the shapes and in areas of vermicelli pattern, both to secure and embellish the appliqué.

TRANSFERRING THE DESIGN

Getting the design on to the fabric seems to be the least-favourite task facing any embroiderer. The method depends to a large extent on the nature of the design: whether it is a simple geometric shape or a more intricate pattern. The following methods are easy to carry out and are ideal for machine-embroidery techniques.

Simple shapes

For a design consisting of circles, squares, rectangles or, say, a simple flower shape, cut a thin-card template accurately for each shape you are using. Iron the fabric and place it on a non-slip surface.

Arrange your templates and, using a water- or air-soluble marker pen, dot round the outline of the shape on to the fabric. Press lightly, spacing the dots fairly close together. It is not usually necessary to draw round with a solid, hard line which can prove stubborn to remove later. Using squares or circles, it is easy to mark round one shape, move the template – perhaps overlapping it with the first shape – and mark round again. Very effective border patterns can be developed in this way.

More complex patterns

Draw out your design on paper, using a black felt-tip pen. Place the ironed fabric on top, securing with either pins or masking tape to prevent movement. You should find it possible to see the design through the fabric, even with cotton or calico.

Trace the design through on to the fabric using a water- or air-soluble marker pen as described earlier. Repeat patterns can be transferred easily by this method, moving the paper design along underneath the fabric as each section is marked. When using a heavier fabric, it may be necessary to tape the design on to a window with the fabric taped on top: the light shining through will make the design easier to follow. A glass-topped coffee table with a small table lamp placed underneath will also serve the purpose.

When all the stitching is complete, remove the marked dotted line by dabbing with a clean, damp cloth.

Intricate designs

Perhaps your chosen design consists of intricate shapes and fine lines which would be impossible to transfer with the relatively thick line of the soluble marker pen. If this is the case, trace your design on to tissue paper. Position this on the fabric, securing it at the edges with a few tacking stitches. Place the fabric and tissue paper into a ring frame, being careful not to tear the tissue.

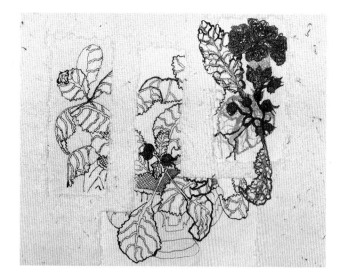

Panel worked mainly in free running stitch, with applied flower and leaves, worked on water-soluble fabric. The design is split into three parts and mounted under hand-made paper (Frances Manz).

Set your machine for free running stitch with a thread similar to the colour of the fabric. Stitch as carefully as you can along the traced lines on the paper. Remove from the frame and tear away the tissue paper (tweezers may be necessary to remove the little bits caught by the stitching). This machined line can then be followed, covered and enhanced by further lines of stitching in your chosen colours for the design.

Do not worry if you find it difficult to follow the design line exactly. Machine embroidery should have spontaneity, which is part of its charm and character. Often two or three lines of stitching around a shape will look better than one hesitant and faltering line, so if your first attempt is a little 'off the mark', go round again and the combination of the two will look even better.

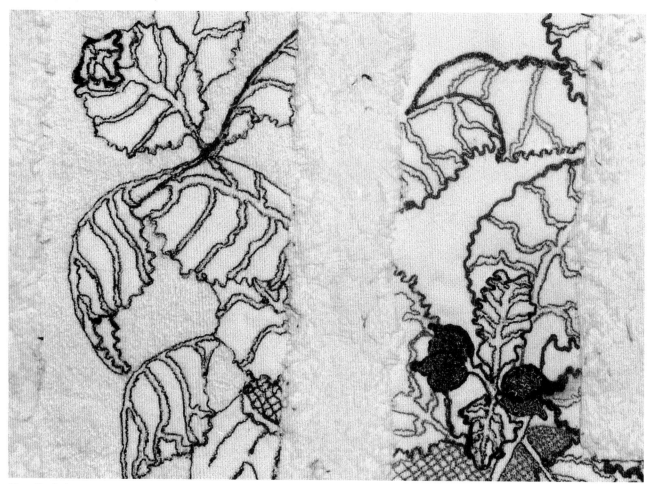

Detail of above.

Dense free running stitch worked on tights, cut out and applied to cotton fabric.

MACHINING ON TIGHTS

By now you should be feeling a little more confident and relaxed about free machine embroidery on ordinary fabrics. Try this experiment. Most of us have access to an endless supply of old tights or stockings which can be used as a base fabric for some very exciting embroidery effects. The only proviso for success is that they must be stretched very, very tightly in the frame before machining on them.

Put the outer ring of the frame down the leg. Devise your own method of clamping one end of the leg against the side of a table whilst pulling hard at the other end, before inserting the inner ring. You

definitely need a second pair of hands for this! Continue to pull and stretch until the tights are drum-tight in the frame. Cut away the rest of the tights around the frame.

Set your machine for free running stitch, remembering to hold both ends of the threads when you start to embroider. Work areas of fairly dense stitching in circles, squares or other simple shapes. Remove the frame from the machine.

Using small, sharp scissors, cut out the shapes as closely as possible to the edge of the stitching. The resulting pieces of embroidery are soft and very flexible with curling edges. Many different effects and degrees of distortion can be achieved by varying the density of the stitching within the shape. Basic flower shapes (as illustrated overleaf) suddenly look quite exotic, with many uses for appliqué, fashion, jewellery and accessories.

To transfer the design of, say, a flower shape on to the tights, it is essential to have them stretched beforehand. Frame the tights as previously described and place over an outline drawing of the shape required. Trace on to the tights using a water- or air-soluble marker. (It does not really matter what colour the tights are as this is virtually invisible when the embroidery is completed.) As well as achieving a wonderful, fun effect, it is satisfying to recycle a waste product too!

Simple flower shapes to be worked on tights to give curling, three-dimensional shapes (see page 21).

APPLIQUÉ

ApplIQUÉ, the technique of applying one fabric on to another, is particularly suitable for the addition of machine embroidery, both to secure the applied pieces and to add extra decoration. It gives a purpose and a structure to the stitching, overcoming the daunting sight of a vast area of plain fabric.

Commercially produced appliqué for fashion and furnishings usually relies on satin stitch to cover the edges of the applied pieces, but this chapter will give you many more ideas for both practical and decorative items.

USING *BONDAWEB*

Many of the following sections will recommend the use of *Bondaweb*, the iron-on adhesive made by Vilene (Pellon). This has been used by embroiderers for many years, but here are some suggestions for those who have not used it before, together with ideas for making the most of the product.

Bondaweb is used to fuse or stick two fabrics together. This prevents the applied piece from moving or puckering while you add the stitching

which further secures it. This ensures a really hard-wearing, washable piece of embroidery.

Bondaweb is clean and easy to use, working well on the vast majority of fabrics. It is available in small packs in the haberdashery department of stores, craft and needlework shops and can also be bought by the metre in larger stores and through specialist suppliers. It looks and feels like paper, with one side smooth and the other textured or rough. There are two basic ways to use *Bondaweb*, depending on the nature of the shape to be applied.

1 If you have a simple or geometric shape, draw or trace this on the smooth side of the paper. Cut out the paper shapes accurately, placing them rough-(adhesive) side down on the fabric to be used for the appliqué. Iron, using firm, even pressure.

Cut out exactly on the edge of each shape, peel off the backing paper and place in position on the background fabric. Make sure that the slightly sticky side (where the paper was) is in contact with the base fabric. Iron in place. Be warned, that if you

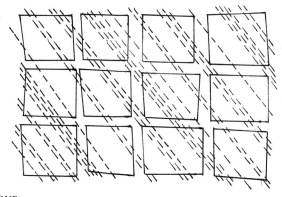

accidentally place a piece the other way up, it will secure itself firmly to the base of your iron!

2 For intricate shapes, or where you want to appliqué a particular area of a patterned fabric, cut a piece of *Bondaweb* larger than the shape to be applied. Draw or trace your design on to the paper side. The design will appear in reverse when applied, so you must reverse your drawing before tracing. This is particularly important if lettering features in the design. Placing the *Bondaweb* rough-side down, iron on to the fabric to be applied.

If you are applying a patterned fabric, carefully select the area you wish to use. With pointed scissors, cut out the intricate design or chosen area of pattern. Peel off the paper backing, place in position on the background fabric and iron in place. With a little experience, other ways of using *Bondaweb* will be discovered. Some of these are explained in the following chapters, where appropriate to a particular technique.

ABOVE:
Grid patterns with ideas for lines of stitching to secure the applied pieces.

BELOW:
The back of the embroidery, showing the method of moving from shape to shape when applying small pieces of fabric.

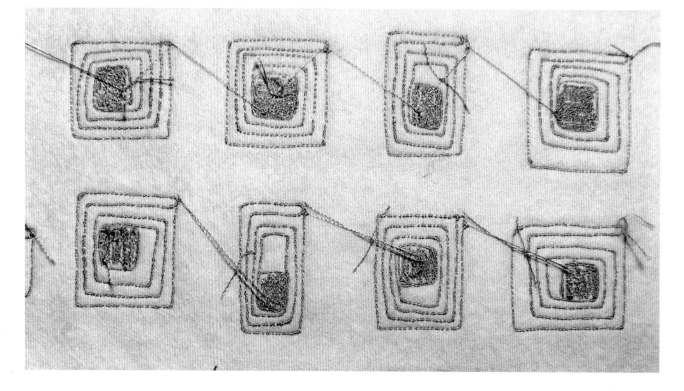

PLAIN FABRICS

Look through your collection of plain fabrics, noting whether they fray easily, have a different surface texture on the right and wrong side, or if they are 'shot' – that is, with weft threads of one colour and warp threads of a different colour.

Plan a simple grid pattern of small squares or rectangles of fabric, each to be held in place with a pattern of free running stitch. Perhaps you could use cream silk and calico together, or alternate the right and wrong sides of a dupion fabric. It is helpful to anchor the pieces in place with *Bondaweb* before adding the stitching, as described in the previous section.

Cut a large square of each of the fabrics to be used, and iron *Bondaweb* to the wrong sides. Cut into strips and then cut the strips into small squares or rectangles. It is not necessary to mark these as exact

Massed short lengths of thread applied to a background fabric, covering it completely. These are secured with lines of narrow satin stitch using a gold metallic thread.

shapes – a certain irregularity adds interest to the final effect. Arrange these on the background fabric and, when you are happy with the arrangement, peel off the backing paper and iron carefully in place. Frame the fabric and it is now ready for the embroidery.

If you wish, you can add a piece of felt behind the background fabric which will give a very slightly quilted effect with the stitching sinking into the fabric. Set your machine for free running stitch, stitching round each applied piece with several lines, using one of the ideas shown on page 32 or your own variation. If the applied pieces fray easily, try fraying

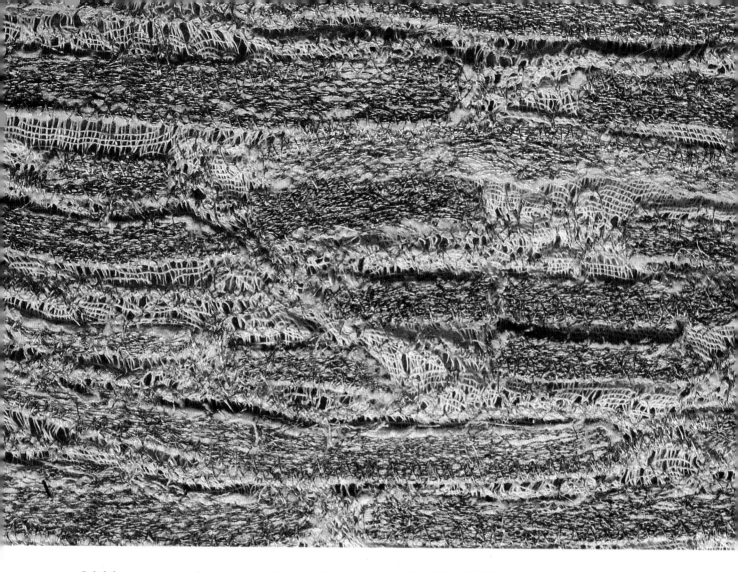

Solid free running stitch worked on calico and felt, bonded together, using a variegated metallic thread. This was cut up into small strips, applied to muslin and secured with free zigzag stitching.

the edges back to the outer line of stitching, this being particularly effective with shot-silk fabrics.

It is not necessary to remove the work from the machine to cut the threads between each stitched square. When you have completed one square, lift the presser-foot lever and pull a loop of approximately 10 cm (4 in.) of the top thread to the side, cutting it in half. Gently move the frame to the position of the next square, easing the bobbin thread as you go, lower the presser-foot lever and start stitching again.

The top threads can be taken to the back of the work, to be tied off when all the stitching has been completed. This not only saves a great deal of time, but will also ensure a neat and hard-wearing finish for items which are likely to undergo a certain amount of wear and tear.

PATTERNED FABRICS

The technique of applying a motif from a patterned fabric to another fabric has been used for many centuries. Some of the lovely furnishing fabrics available today are particularly suitable for this technique.

Choose the fabric with care, imagining how easy – or difficult – it will be to cut out the motifs and how you can best arrange them on a background fabric. Many flower designs are perfect for this, but not, of course, little sprigs or very intricate shapes. Iron *Bondaweb* to the wrong side of the chosen area of the patterned fabric, cutting out the motifs carefully. Arrange these in groups, bands or all-over patterns.

It is worthwhile, at this stage, taking time to consider how the added stitching will affect the design. Place the motifs on a large piece of paper and roughly sketch in where you anticipate adding embroidery. When you are happy with the arrangement, place the motifs on the background fabric, removing the paper backing. Iron in place.

Set your machine for free running stitch and frame the fabric. Work lines of stitching just inside the cut edges of each shape, continuing round and round with contour lines on the background fabric. Sooner or later, these lines will meet up with the lines going round an adjoining shape, and a new pattern will emerge. Do not worry if your lines of stitching are not perfectly parallel with the previous line. This slight irregularity adds to the charm of the pattern.

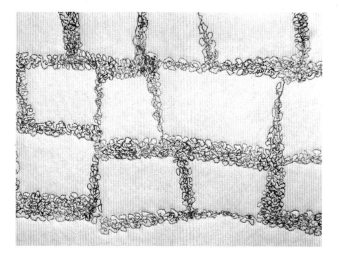

RIGHT:
The back of an embroidery, showing vermicelli stitch worked over, and between, applied shapes.

Detail of appliqué panel. The small squares were secured with an automatic machine pattern (Gillian Ghibaldan).

Squares of free running stitch worked on tights, with various shades of pink and gold thread on the spool and green on the bobbin. These were cut out and applied to green cotton fabric.

An alternative to contour lines of stitching around the shapes is to use vermicelli, a close meandering pattern of free running stitch (see previous page, top). Use this to cover the raw edges of the shape, shadowing parts of the background areas as you wish. Both these methods of stitching help to unite the applied pieces with the background fabric. An attractive use of vermicelli as a background 'filler' is to arrange circles, squares or other simple shapes with small spaces between them.

Try making your own patterned fabric by sponging fabric paint on to a plain fabric, or use an all-over abstract pattern for the appliqué. Cover the edges of each shape, and the spaces between, with vermicelli. This can be particularly effective using a shaded or variegated thread.

BURNT EDGES

Not all appliqué needs to have a smooth-cut edge. Some fabrics, particularly silks, look delightful with a singed or burnt edge. Apply *Bondaweb* to the back of a piece of silk, cut out a strip or other shape (which should not be too small or fiddly), leaving the paper backing in place.

Place a candle, firmly supported, on a piece of old board, making sure there are no draughts. Touch the edges of the fabric, slowly and carefully, into the side of the flame. Have an old cloth to hand to put out any flames which continue to burn on the fabric. Work along the edge, a little at a time, just sealing the ends of the fibres.

Please *be very careful* to observe sensible safety precautions when trying this, especially if using synthetic fabrics which can flare up alarmingly. Dust off excessive charring, peel off the backing paper and iron in place on to the background fabric.

This irregular burnt edge looks best with freely worked 'irregular' stitching. Try two or three lines around each shape, making little jerks in the stitching and letting the lines cross over each other

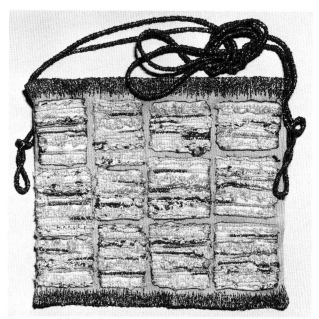

Squares of felt and calico, bonded together with lines of free stitching and couched threads. The edges of the squares were burnt before being applied to the background with free running stitch.

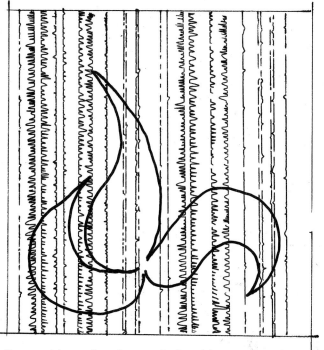

Suggested lines of stitching worked on fabric, prior to the motif being cut out and used for appliqué.

and the burnt edges at random. This is definitely a case for enjoying the haphazard stitching which tends to plague the inexperienced!

DECORATED FABRICS

Many fabrics can be pre-stitched with embroidery before being cut to shape and used for appliqué. This can give added texture and interest to what is essentially a flat technique. It is an ideal opportunity to try out all those utility stitches and automatic patterns which are a feature of many modern machines – often little used!

Massed lines of zigzag with different width and length settings, using a variegated thread, can be very attractive. This stitching would, of course, be worked with the machine set for ordinary sewing. One of the most effective techniques is to work lines of twin-needle stitching or pin tucking, the instructions for which will be found in your machine manual.

When all the stitching is complete, cut out the shapes required for the appliqué. Do not worry about cutting across the lines of stitching. The cut ends of the threads will be secured when the piece is applied to the background fabric. The little bag illustrated shows this technique to great effect.

Small bag with pin tucking on organza shapes, applied to silk fabric with added stitchery, appliqué and beads (Celia Litchfield-Dunn).

Leaves and flowers outlined with free running stitch on organza, cut out, and applied to a painted and printed background (Gillian Ghibaldan).

APPLIQUÉ ON BACKGROUND FABRICS

It is often presumed that appliqué is only used for the design itself. This can be reversed so that the background fabric of the piece has the appliqué, over which the design is stitched.

Many embroiderers have a collection of nets and sheer fabrics which can be torn into strips and overlapped on a base fabric. Silk net can be found in the bridal department of many large stores and this is infinitely preferable to the nylon net which is more widely available. Silk net can be dyed in soft, muted colours and tears beautifully. Use tints, tones and shades of one colour or, perhaps, your own sponged or dyed fabrics. This will give a shaded, dappled background which will be perfect for an embroidered line design.

Sometimes a slightly thicker line of stitching will be needed to 'show up' on the appliquéd background. Try the narrowest possible satin-stitch width setting – just enough to throw the needle from side to side. Worked closely, as free stitching, this

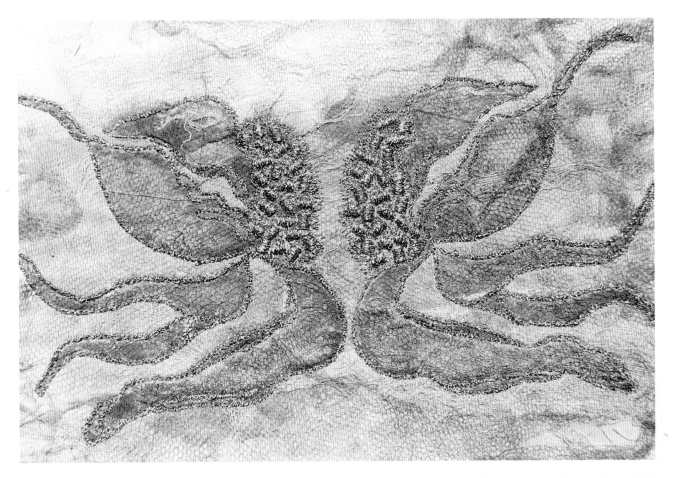

Torn strips of muslin and nets bonded to the background, with a design based on roses worked in very narrow free satin stitch. Parts of the design were then painted.

gives a very attractive textured line.

Depending on the nature of the design you choose, extra stitching on the background may be required to secure the pieces, or they can be bonded in place. If you use *Bondaweb* with sheer fabrics, always place a piece of baking parchment (or the discarded, peeled-off backing paper from *Bondaweb*) over the work before ironing, otherwise the adhesive will come through the sheer fabrics on to the base of your iron. In a purely decorative embroidery, you can leave the torn, unsecured edges as part of the overall effect.

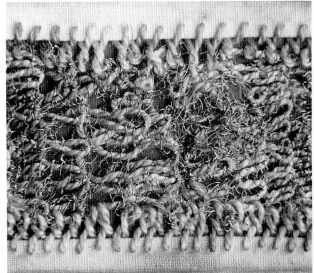

Space-dyed threads laid at random on water-soluble fabric, and secured with free stitching using a copper metallic thread. The band is held with hand-worked insertion stitches and mounted under a frame of space-dyed fabric (Frances Manz).

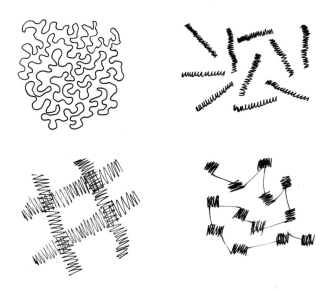

Patterns of stitches used to hold applied threads in place.

Bag made with a fabric composed of medium-weight threads, held side by side with free running stitch and finished with a twisted cord (Jenny Dench).

MASSED THREADS

Instead of the usual fabric appliqué, it is possible to cover the surface of a background fabric with applied threads. At first glance, this may not seem a very practical idea, but it can be surprisingly hard-wearing, depending on the amount of stitching used to secure the threads. To make the stitching easier, it is helpful to anchor or secure the threads to the fabric backing.

Cut a square of *Bondaweb* and carefully peel off the paper backing, leaving the fine adhesive mesh. Place this on the backing fabric (it does not matter which way up – it is now 'adhesive' on both sides). Cover with threads in a variety of ways:

1   fairly thick, smooth threads laid evenly side by side.
2   textured yarns, laid regularly or in a random pattern.
3   threads pulled from fabric and cut into short lengths.
4   embroidery threads, perhaps variegated or shaded. Hold the loose ends of a number of reels of thread, cutting the bundle into short lengths.
5   synthetic, multi-coloured fleece.
6   teased-out quilting wool.

It is essential to cover the adhesive mesh completely with threads before ironing. As a precaution, cover

Frame with area for a small mirror or photograph. The design is worked separately on water-soluble fabric with machine-wrapped cords and applied to the background fabric (Linda Cook).

the work with baking parchment or the discarded paper backing of a used piece of *Bondaweb*. Peel off immediately after ironing. If you require a really hard-wearing finish, or if you do not wish to cover the backing fabric completely, cover the whole area with a sheer fabric such as chiffon or organza, but still use the paper cover when ironing.

The stitching can be worked in a toning or contrasting colour in any of the following ways:

1   an openly-worked vermicelli.
2   short lines of satin stitch, worked at different angles.
3   lines of open zigzag.
4   automatic patterns.
5   satin-stitch blobs. Stitching almost on the spot with satin stitch, making a little raised bead of stitching.

Suggested patterns of stitching to be worked on tights.

APPLIED STITCHING

On page 29, instructions are given for machining on tights or stockings. These small pieces of solid stitching can be used for appliqué, having the advantage of being very soft and flexible. Work a number of squares or circles, changing either the top or bobbin thread to give subtle colour changes. It is a great advantage to be able to move these pieces around before deciding on the final arrangement on the backing fabric. They can also be pulled to a new shape, rolled or distorted before stitching down.

Use free running stitch to anchor them in place, either over the edges or within the shape. The latter method allows the edges to curl up.

A little imagination – and a pile of little squares – will soon conjure up new ways of applying them. Try adding a little padding behind each square to give an effect of trapunto quilting. Shapes can be overlapped, or smaller shapes placed over larger ones.

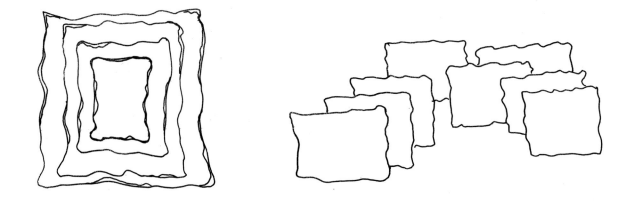

Examples of how the stitched pieces can be arranged.

Detail of log-cabin silk cushion, showing quilted design of roses worked in free running stitch with applied areas, worked on water-soluble fabric.

Detail of cushion. Hand-sewn hexagon patchwork painted along the seam lines with silk paints and quilted with free running stitch.

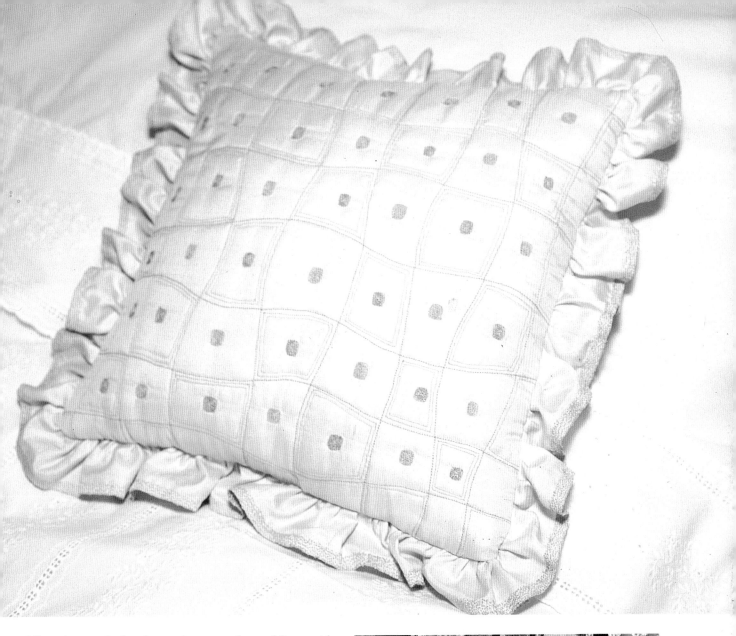

Silk cushion quilted with a grid pattern of curved lines, with small squares of solid free running stitch in the centres. The frill is edged with a band of free running stitch, worked at right angles to the folded edge.

Detail of hat. Hand and machine appliqué, with detached shapes worked with solid free machining (Margaret Ross). The complete hat is shown on page 85.

Solid free running stitch worked on bonded calico and felt, cut up and applied with extra free stitching (Annette Monks).

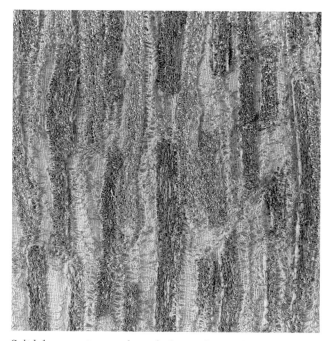

Solid free running stitch worked on calico and felt, bonded together, using metallic threads. This was cut up and applied to muslin with free zigzag stitch.

CUTTING UP SOLID STITCHING

Work solid free running stitch on a firm base of calico and felt. Held together with *Bondaweb*, this makes an ideal surface on which to stitch, strong enough to support even the densest stitching. Work with the calico side uppermost. Try putting two threads together in the needle using free running stitch. Variegated and metallic threads look particularly attractive, with the colours blending together to make a mottled pattern.

When you have stitched an area really solidly – so that no background fabric remains visible – take the scissors and cut it up into little strips, perhaps 2·5 to 5 cm (an inch or two) long. This seems strange, but may solve the problem of what to do with a piece of stitching which has gone slightly wrong!

Apply these strips to a background of muslin using free zigzag stitch, both to secure the pieces in place as well as covering part or all of the cut edges. Use the point of a stiletto or a small screwdriver to hold them in place while you catch them in the stitching. The zigzag stitch will pull the muslin into a free pulled-fabric effect, which contrasts beautifully with the solid pieces.

OLD EMBROIDERIES

Many of us are lucky enough to have a collection of old embroideries and lace which are treasured heirlooms of a previous age. Old whitework embroidery, meticulously worked table-cloths and household linens are kept for special occasions perhaps, but what can be done with fragments or badly worn items, no longer usable?

Often it is the fabric of the item which has perished or is badly stained, whereas the embroidery remains in good condition. Cut out the sound embroidery and apply it to a background of organdie or fine cotton in a random or geometric patchwork-type pattern. Satin stitch can be used to secure the cut edges, and added embroidery worked to unite the whole.

It is very satisfying to salvage these marvellous examples of fine needlework, making cushions, hangings or modern-day runners or table-cloths. It would be sacrilege, however, to cut up an article of historic interest in good condition. This suggestion is purely a means of enjoying a fragment of old embroidery, otherwise destined to live, unappreciated, in a drawer for ever.

Dressing-table runner. Fragments of old whitework embroideries applied with added free satin stitch and running stitch.

Detail of the above.

Detail of cushion. Frayed, woven strips of silk fabric are quilted with free running stitch in a pattern of rectangles formed by the weaving process.

LEAVES AND FLOWERS

Frame a sheer fabric such as organza or organdie, setting your machine for free running stitch. Work around the outline shape of leaves and flowers, adding stitching to define vein or inner-petal lines and centres. Remove from the frame, cutting out each shape with sharp, fine-pointed scissors as near to the outer line of stitching as possible.

Work a selection in close tones of one colour, both in fabric and thread. These can be built up into areas of very attractive, decorative appliqué for hangings and pictures.

Attach with free running stitch at the base of a leaf or through the centre of a flower, securing as much or as little of the shape as you wish. This is especially attractive if the background fabric has also been printed with leaves and flowers, the applied shapes adding extra texture for the focal point of the design.

3

QUILTING

Throughout history, quilting has been a popular technique for fashion items, accessories and home furnishings. It is basically a sandwich of two fabrics with padding between them, the layers held together with stitching.

All forms of quilting offer scope for machine embroidery. It is often an advantage to work stitching on more than one layer of fabric, and the padding eliminates any tendency for the work to appear puckered. Machine embroidery seems to sink into the fabric far more than hand stitching. This highlights the main characteristic of quilting, which is the contrast between the stitched areas or lines and the soft, raised, padded parts of the design.

ENGLISH QUILTING

This requires a top fabric, a backing fabric and a layer of wadding between the two. A fine, closely woven top fabric will give the best results. Silk is an ideal choice, as the sheen of the fabric catches the light and enhances the contrast between the stitching and the plain fabric.

Polyester quilting wadding (batting) is widely available in 2 oz, 4 oz and 8 oz weights, with the purpose of the article determining the thickness of wadding required. Pieces of wadding can be used together to provide thicker layers. 2 oz wadding is a good weight to use for most articles. Pre-washed felt is an alternative. It gives a slightly padded effect to the stitching and usually requires no backing fabric. When using polyester wadding, a backing fabric is needed, and this can be muslin, fine calico or old well-washed sheeting.

Mark the design on to the top fabric before putting the layers together. A simple all-over pattern is ideal to begin with. Irregular curved lines can be drawn with the help of a French curve (available from most art shops), or torn paper strips can be used as a template guide. Draw the lines lightly on to the fabric using a water- or air-soluble pen. For a larger area of quilting, it is quite easy to machine the lines freely without the aid of a marked line.

A simple design can be printed on to the fabric using fabric paints, with the quilting line following

ABOVE: *Zigzag stitch, worked sideways in a pattern of squares, completely covering the fabric. Half of each square is worked in a textured metallic thread, the other half in a rayon thread. A thin metallic ribbon is couched by machine between the squares.*

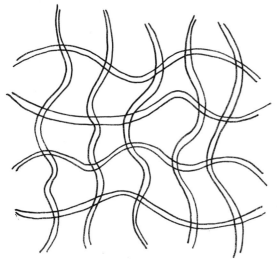

Pattern of curved lines suitable for quilting.

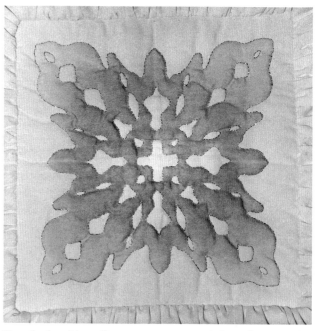

Detail of cushion. Design sponge-printed through a stencil and quilted with metallic thread (Celia Litchfield-Dunn).

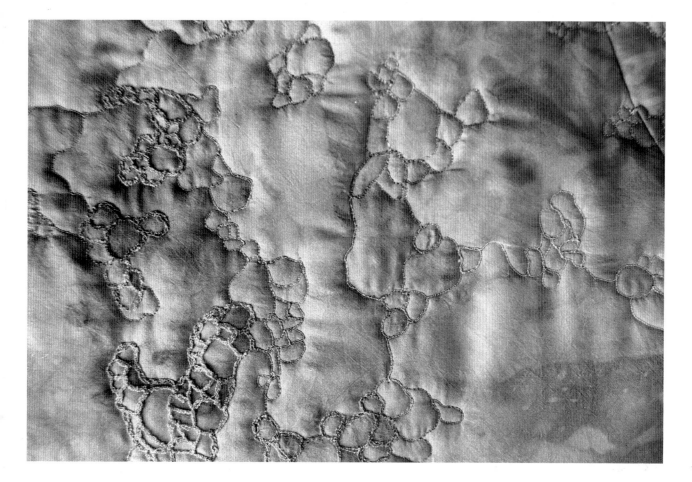

ABOVE:
*Detail of a quilted jacket made of space-dyed silk fabric.
Parts of the embroidery are worked on water-soluble fabric,
applied with added free running stitch (Celia
Litchfield-Dunn).*

RIGHT:
*Small bag with design based on zebra-coat patterns. Black
silk applied to white velvet using free running stitch with a
silver metallic thread (Annette Monks).*

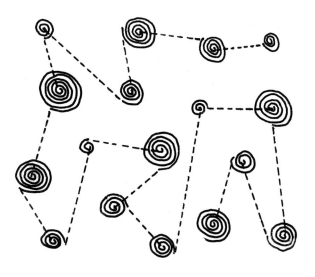

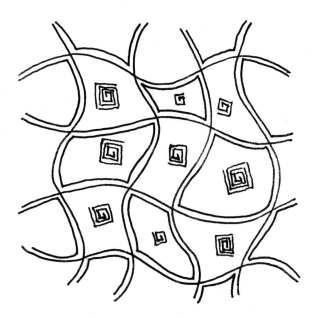

Quilting patterns.

the outlines of the pattern. The inspiration for this could be taken from a tile, mosaic floor or a motif on curtain or upholstery fabric. Although it takes a little time to cut a stencil accurately from thin card for the design, it is time well spent. Place the stencil on the fabric, securing with masking tape, and sponge colour on to the fabric.

Place the three layers together – top fabric, wadding and backing fabric – and tack vertical and horizontal lines about 5 cm (2 in.) apart to keep everything in place. Set your machine for free running stitch, choosing a thread to match either the colour of the background fabric or the printed design. Use the darning foot.

Hold the fabrics firmly, stretching them as taut as you can while stitching along the lines. Work two or three lines of stitching close together to add emphasis to the pattern. For more intricate areas of the design, it is a great help to frame the work, as well as using the darning foot. The frame keeps the fabric taut, is easy to hold and allows you to concentrate on the stitching.

Quilting designs do not have to be composed of lines. Try working small, dense areas of stitching – perhaps circles or squares – at random over the surface. This would be a variation of the hand technique of tied quilting. It could be used on its own or in conjunction with a line pattern.

Detail of jacket. Free running stitch with a variegated thread on space-dyed fabric (Linda Cook).

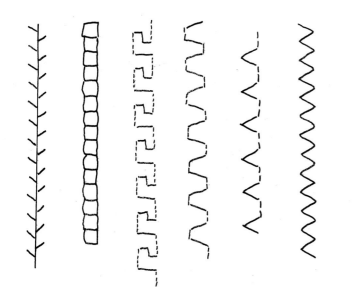

A selection of the automatic patterns to be found on many modern sewing machines.

AUTOMATIC PATTERNS

Many modern machines have a range of utility and automatic patterns which can be used for English quilting. In the sample shown overleaf, the top fabric, a fine calico, was printed with a simple design of lines and squares. A piece of sponge was cut to shape, dabbed first into the fabric paint, then on to the fabric, making a grid pattern. Diagonal lines were added with a 2·5 cm (1 in.) household paint brush used very dry. Just touch the ends of the bristles into the paint and stroke lightly over the fabric.

Prepare the three layers as previously described and tack together. Work lines of automatic patterns using the machine set up for ordinary sewing. Many of these patterns offer scope for threading thick yarns through the stitches (by hand, of course) using a tapestry needle. This gives a rich, braided effect using stitches such as raised-chain band, Pekinese stitch, interlaced band or laced running stitch.

Composite stitches to be laced by hand on to a base of an automatic machine pattern. From the top: laced running stitch, Pekinese stitch, interlaced band and raised-chain band.

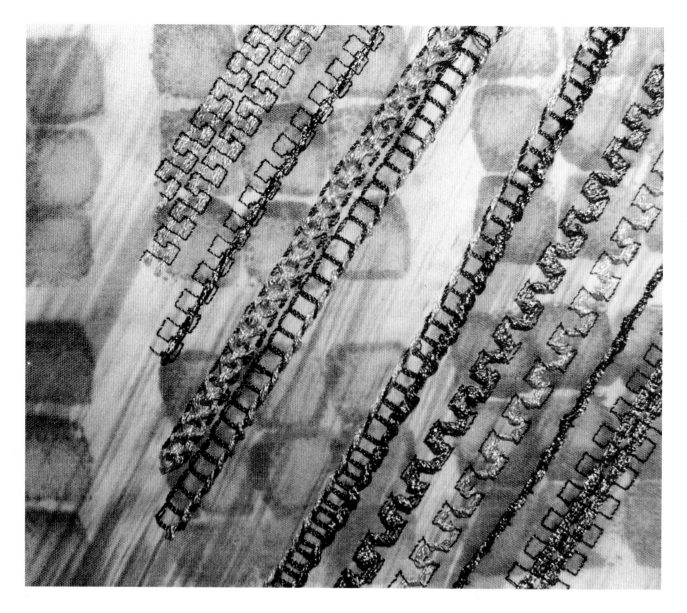

Automatic machine patterns quilted on to a sponge-printed background, laced with fine metallic braids, cords and ribbons.

A glance at a book on hand stitches will give many more possibilities. There is an increasingly good selection of metallic braids and fine ribbon threads on the market now. These would give a very rich effect threaded through automatic pattern quilting for an evening bag.

Free-running-stitch contour quilting on a flower-patterned satin fabric.

CONTOUR QUILTING

This is a simple and very effective form of English quilting, with free running stitch worked around the outlines of a patterned fabric. Choose the fabric with care, as some degree of continuity is required within the pattern outlines. Very small shapes or isolated flower sprigs are not really suitable; an overall design, whether naturalistic or geometric, is ideal.

Matching the colour of thread to the predominant colour in the fabric, work free running stitch around the shapes. It is helpful to frame the work (the patterned fabric, wadding and backing fabric) especially if the design is fairly complex. There is great scope in this technique for home furnishings and fashion ideas. Quilt the fabric for a pelmet and tie-backs to make luxurious curtains, or a waistcoat, jacket or bag to co-ordinate with a garment made in the patterned fabric.

Quilting design taken from patterned fabric.

Silk fabric painted in streaks with pink-and-green silk paints. Bands of free running stitch are worked with two threads in the needle, leaving varying-width bands of Italian quilting between them. The cushion is finished with a frill, edged with free running stitch.

QUILTED HEXAGON PATCHWORK

Hand-sewn hexagon patchwork is a technique which most embroiderers have tried at some time. However, it is not often seen as a machine-quilted technique, combined with fabric printing.

Work an area of hexagons as described in any book on patchwork, using a plain, closely woven fabric. Again, silk is ideal, but you could use a fine, pre-washed cotton, calico or cotton-and-polyester-mixture fabric.

Before you embark on the patchwork, test a piece of the chosen fabric with fabric paint to see if the effect is going to be attractive. Just dip a fine paint brush into the fabric paint (the type sold as silk paint is ideal), stroking it on to the fabric. It should 'bleed'

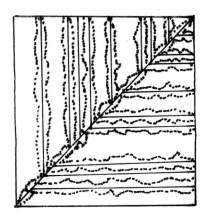
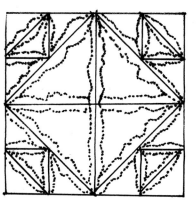

An American patchwork block and a strip-pieced block, showing how they could be enhanced with fabric paints along the seam lines.

gently sideways, giving neither a thin line, nor a flood! Much of this effect can be controlled by the amount of paint on your brush and by how firmly you press. Damp fabric also encourages the bleeding process.

When the patchwork is complete, remove the tacking and press with an iron, but leave the papers in place. Choose two or three colours of fabric paint. Brush each colour in turn into the seam lines, allowing the colours to blend into each other and out into the surrounding fabric. Do not be tempted to save time by painting all the blobs of one colour first, followed by the second and third colours. The paint dries very quickly and the merging colour effect will be lost.

When completely dry, iron to set the colours as described on the fabric-paint instructions. Prepare the three layers necessary for English quilting and secure in a ring frame. Set the machine for free running stitch, choosing a colour to blend with the fabric painting. Stitch round within each hexagon shape, following the wiggly line where the paint stopped bleeding.

This combined fabric-painting and machine-quilting technique could be used for many other types of patchwork, such as strip patchwork, American blocks or other geometric shapes. Some very exciting colour effects can be imagined by working patchwork in a variety of plain-coloured fabrics (or even patterned fabrics) with the added colour dimension of fabric painting in the seam lines.

Rose designs to be quilted on to a base of log-cabin patchwork.

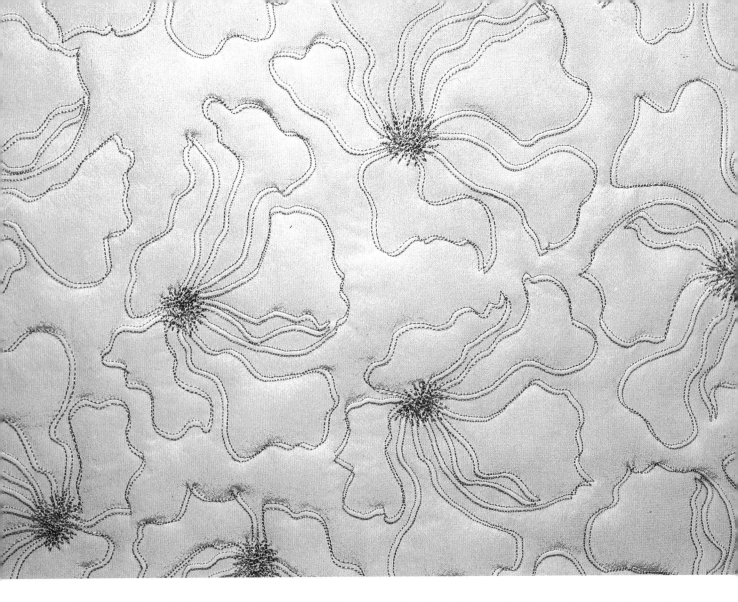

QUILTED LOG-CABIN PATCHWORK

Log cabin is usually quilted at the piecing stage or by the addition of straight lines following the strips. An alternative is to prepare the log-cabin block, backed on to a very fine butter muslin, adding a quilted design as a separate element. Choose a limited colour range for the patchwork: perhaps just a couple of fairly plain fabrics, or the right and wrong sides of a dupion furnishing fabric.

After the log-cabin block has been worked, transfer the quilting design using a water- or air-soluble marker pen. Prepare the sandwich of three layers, tack together, and place in a ring frame. Set your machine for free running stitch and work along the lines of the design. You could, perhaps, choose a motif traced from curtain material or a wallpaper pattern. Look for a fairly simple outline shape – flowers, butterflies, birds or leaf shapes would be ideal.

Detail of silk crêpe de Chine cushion. The design of roses is quilted with a twin needle, giving a pin-tucked line that resembles an italic pen.

FRAYED WOVEN STRIPS

It is necessary to choose a fabric which frays easily for this technique; otherwise it can seem a very tedious process! Check first that your fabric has been cut with the straight grain and, if not, do this first. Mark lines along the fabric, using log-cabin markers or the width of a ruler, approximately 5 cm (2 in.) apart. This can be varied to suit particular purposes.

Cut the strips and fray out each side. You will need a square of fine backing fabric, and it is helpful to place this on an old cork mat or sheet of hard polyester foam. Lay the strips of fabric, side by side, with the edges of the fringe just touching. Pin in place at each end of each strip. When the backing fabric has been completely covered in this way, take more strips, placing these at right angles, and weave them through the previously laid strips in an 'over and under' pattern. Again, pin at both ends of each strip.

To stabilize the work before the quilting process, it is worthwhile tacking along all four sides, through the ends of the strips and on to the backing fabric. This can now be prepared for quilting as described earlier. Setting your machine for free running stitch, work small squares within the plain fabric areas. The stitching sinks into the fabric, emphasizing the fringed edges. Although this technique looks delicate, the quilting lines secure the fringing, making it fairly hard-wearing for cushions or bags.

Bath towel, hand towel and face cloth embroidered with a pattern of circles in free running stitch. (See pages 65–7 for details.)

ZIGZAG QUILTING

As well as the more usual free running stitch for quilting, it is possible to use free zigzag stitch too. This is very effective worked sideways as a dense stitched area, instead of just lines of open zigzag or satin stitch.

Try a small practice piece. Frame a fabric, setting your machine for free satin stitch with the maximum-width stitch. The feed dog should be lowered or covered and you may like to use the darning foot as well. Check that the swing of the needle from side to side is within the width of your darning foot by turning the fly wheel carefully by hand towards you for a couple of stitches. You can, of course, work with no foot in place, making sure that the fabric is taut in the frame.

Start stitching, moving the frame from side to side. The stitches will overlap and encroach, building to give a lovely textured effect. This can be worked on a sandwich of top and backing fabric, with wadding in-between, but will require some areas of fabric to be left unstitched to provide the contrasting 'quilted' effect.

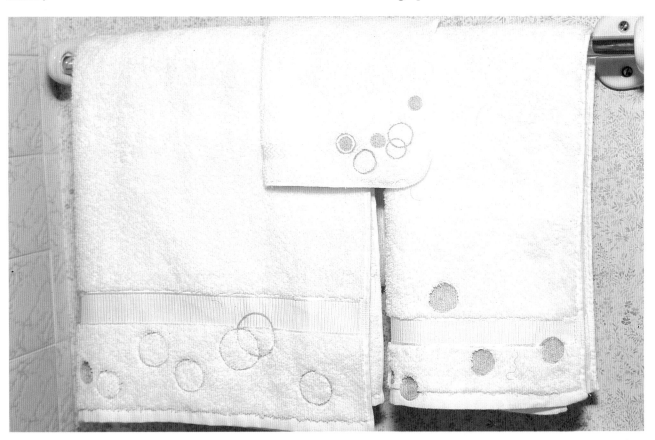

Folded-triangle patchwork using cream silk and calico, with satin stitch worked in a variegated thread.

Try this alternative method. Draw a grid pattern of squares or rectangles on fabric. Place in a frame and fill each of the shapes with completely dense or solid sideways zigzag. Try one of the crinkly textured metallic threads for this. Many people find these difficult to use for free running stitch but they are almost foolproof when used for sideways zigzag. Just remember to use a larger size needle and reduce the top tension considerably – this also adds to the loopy, textured surface.

When all the shapes have been filled with stitching, remove from the frame and place wadding and a backing fabric behind the embroidery. The lines of the grid, between the areas of dense stitching, can now be machined with several lines of running stitch or satin stitch as in ordinary sewing. A narrow ribbon or braid can be sewn in place along the grid lines. Either way, the grid sinks into the wadding, throwing up the stitched squares in relief. Even though the effect is very rich and textured, it is surprisingly quick and easy to work.

FOLDED-TRIANGLE PATCHWORK

This is a hand-sewn technique which can be partly embroidered on the machine, giving an interesting textured or quilted surface. It relies on the fact that if you fold the three points of an equilateral triangle to the centre, a hexagonal shape is formed. Thus it becomes a variation of traditional hexagon patchwork. The diagrams opposite explain the stages of the technique.

1 Cut an equilateral-triangle card template. The length of the sides can be varied, but 10 cm (4 in.) is a good size to start with. Find the exact centre and punch a small hole at this point with a stiletto or leather punch.

2 Choose two fabrics which complement each other in colour and texture. Draw round the

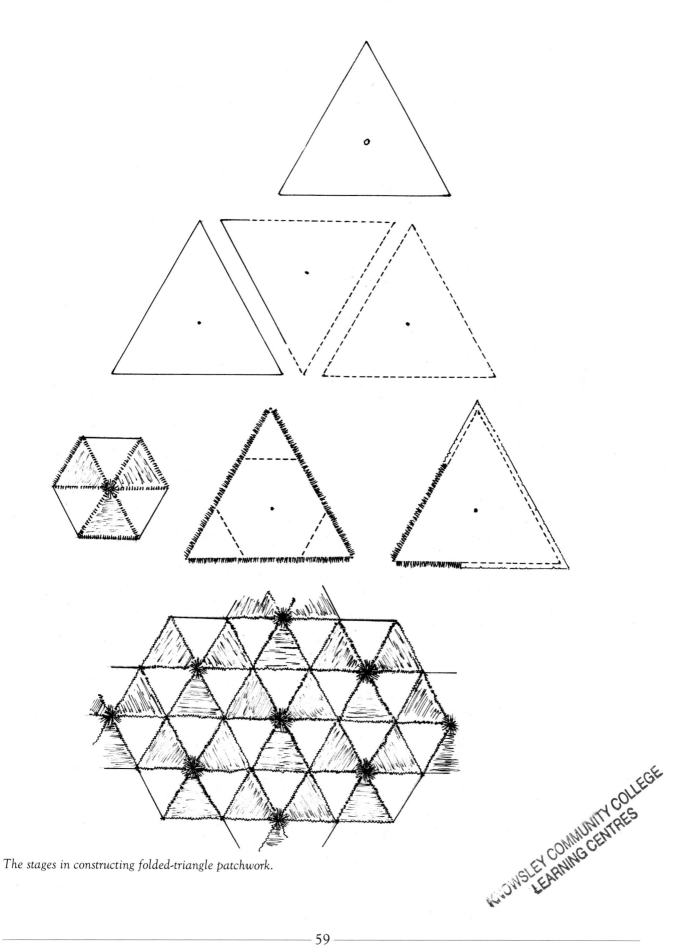

The stages in constructing folded-triangle patchwork.

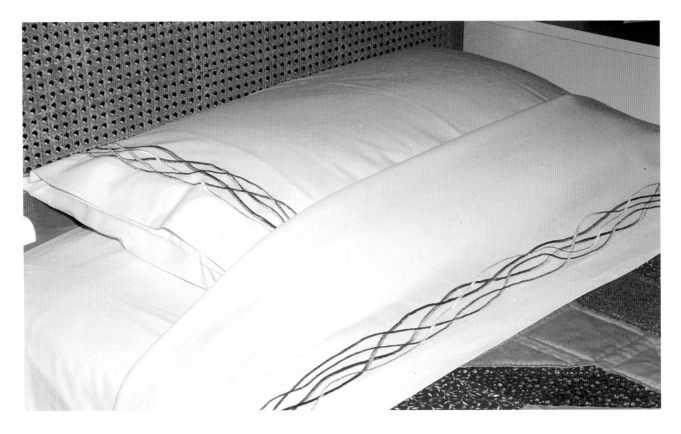

Sheet and pillow case embroidered with a border pattern of curving, crossing lines of satin stitch in varying widths and colours. The stitching was worked in a frame with the ordinary satin-stitch presser foot in place and the feed dog raised. (See pages 68–9 for details.)

template with a pencil on the right side of one of the fabrics. It does not matter which fabric you select for this, so choose the one on which it is easiest to see the drawn line. Mark round the triangles, leaving a small gap between each. Make a dot with a water- or air-soluble marker through the central hole on each triangle.

3   Place the second fabric beneath the first, wrong sides together, with a layer of thin wadding or pre-washed felt between the two.

4   With your machine set for ordinary straight-stitch sewing, stitch along the pencil lines through all layers of fabric.

5   Cut out each triangle, as closely as possible to the stitched lines.

6   Set your machine for ordinary satin stitch and work over the edges of each triangle. You will need to try out various stitch widths and lengths to

achieve the neatest effect. Do not worry too much about the points, as these are covered later.

7   Fold the three points of each triangle to the central marked spot, making a hexagon shape. Catch the points to the centre with a few stitches by hand.

8   If your machine has an eyelet attachment, this can be used to secure and decorate the centre. Alternatively, work an eyelet by hand, or work a small circle of free running stitch on the machine over the central point.

9   The hexagons are now joined by hand, by placing them right sides together and over-casting on the wrong side, as in conventional hand-sewn patchwork.

A variegated thread has been used for the satin stitch and eyelet in the sample illustrated on page 58, with cream-silk and calico fabrics. Metallic thread on rich, dark fabrics would be perfect for a small evening bag.

ITALIAN QUILTING

A glance at illustrations of traditional Italian quilting in books will show two parallel lines of stitching with quilting wool threaded through the resulting channel. The padded lines, and the shadows they create, are the focal point of the technique. In this section, it is the machined areas which form an equal part of the decorative effect.

In all methods of Italian quilting, two layers of material are used: a top fabric and a backing fabric. Traditionally, the backing fabric was always an open muslin, but for the following methods, fine calico or sheeting would be suitable.

Choose a top fabric which is soft and closely woven. Mark a number of parallel lines across the width using a water- or air-soluble marker pen. The lines can be spaced unevenly. Place a backing fabric behind, frame the work, and prepare the machine for free running stitch, either with or without a darning foot.

Hold the frame under the machine with the marked lines running horizontally. Work short lines of free running stitch toward and away from you, with the marked line as your central guide for the band of stitching. If you miss a bit and the fabric shows through the stitching, go back and fill this in with more lines. A shaded or variegated thread looks particularly good, as well as using two threads in the needle together. Work a band of stitching along every line you have marked.

After all the embroidery is completed, thread enough strands of quilting wool through the channels between the stitching to make them nicely padded. Very narrow channels may only need one strand, whereas the thicker channels may need seven

Embroidered duvet cover and pillow case. Some of the printed heart motifs are outlined with free running stitch, with added lines of satin stitch. (See pages 68–70 for details.)

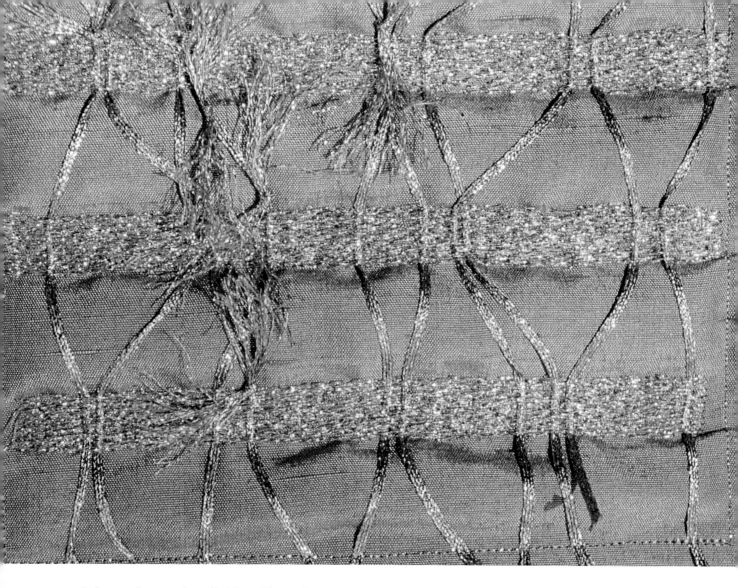

Italian quilting on shot-silk fabric. The stitching is worked in sideways free zigzag using a textured metallic thread. Narrow metallic ribbons are threaded and knotted through the stitching.

or eight. Cut off any protruding ends of the quilting wool. Machine a line of straight stitching along the open channel sides to secure the quilting wool in place. This can now be made up into a cushion or bag.

Blocks of Italian quilting, worked in this way, could be joined together to make a larger item, alternating the channels, vertically and horizontally, on adjoining blocks. This would make an unusual headboard or decorative hanging.

ITALIAN QUILTING WITH ZIGZAG

This is similar to the previous technique, but instead of bands of free running stitch, it is worked with bands of free sideways zigzag stitch. Use two layers of fabric, as before, stitching sideways along the marked areas, and thread quilting wool through the channels between the stitching.

One of the characteristics of this stitch is the somewhat loopy nature of the surface. Use this to advantage by threading braid or thin ribbon through the band of stitching, using a tapestry or blunt needle. Work at right angles to the bands, going through the stitched areas and passing over the padded areas.

Many variations are possible – what you choose to thread through, whether this is done regularly or at random and, of course, the endless possibilities of using subtle or contrasting colours. A metallic braid or ribbon will catch the light, especially as it passes over the padded areas.

TWIN-NEEDLE QUILTING

Twin needles are used for lines of decorative stitching or pin tucks. They will be available from your machine dealer and can be used on virtually every make of machine. They are made in various sizes, with the two needles joined together on one shank.

Used with free running stitch for quilting, some very exciting results can be seen. Imagine that the twin needle is an italic pen. When you stitch towards you and away from you, a double line results, but by moving the fabric from side to side only a single line is visible. The best effects, therefore, will be achieved by stitching in curved and swirling patterns which maximize the 'italic' effect.

Patterns for 'italic-pen' twin-needle quilting.

Space-dyed silk applied to a green fabric. The edges of the appliqué were burnt in a candle flame before being secured with meandering lines of very narrow free satin stitch. The same stitching is worked on the edge of the frill.

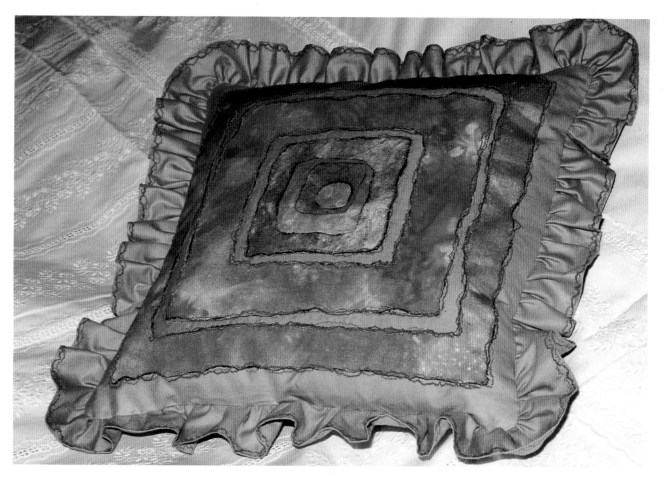

Refer to your manual for precise instructions for fitting a twin needle and threading the machine. You will need two reels of thread on the top of the machine but only one bobbin thread. Try two different colour threads or perhaps two shaded or variegated threads. Fill the bobbin with a colour to match the fabric. A soft fabric such as silk or synthetic crêpe is ideal for this technique, but experiment too with fine lawn or voile. Back the fabric with 2 oz polyester wadding, but no backing fabric.

The next instruction will sound like a mistake, but it really does work best like this! Leave the feed dog up, even though you will be working free running stitch. Frame the fabric and wadding together, using a darning foot if you have one. Machine in swirls, curves and circles. Move the frame up and down and from side to side to see how the italic-pen effect is achieved.

The rose design in the diagram was very easy to work. The centre area was worked with the twin needle, stitching short lines radiating from the centre outwards and back again. This also served to cover the somewhat untidy join area of the petals. The resulting fabric is beautifully soft and flexible. It would be an ideal technique for fashion garments, as it can be lined and made up without the usual stiffness which accompanies many quilted garments. Do try it.

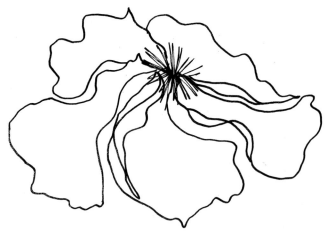

Flower design suitable for twin-needle quilting.

4

EMBROIDERY
FOR THE HOME

I DO not intend to give detailed instructions for the construction of soft furnishings such as lampshades, window blinds or cushions, but rather to suggest decorative embroidery to embellish such items. There are many specialist books written on the technical aspects of soft furnishings which you may care to consult for particular skills.

It is also useful to look through magazines or to visit large department stores and specialist shops noting the current trends in home design. These can inspire many ideas, using your own colour preferences and combinations. There is enormous satisfaction in producing something which adds that special individual touch to a room. Many items are illustrated to give you ideas for bed linen, cushions, curtain tie-backs and so on, using techniques described in earlier chapters.

TOWELS
Towels are usually purchased to complement the colour scheme of a bathroom or cloakroom, but these can rarely pick up the variety of tint, tone and shade in a room. Use the embroidery to emphasize a certain colour or, perhaps, take a motif from the tiles or wallpaper for a border pattern. Intricate designs are not really possible on the textured surface of towelling, so keep the shapes simple.

Begin by practising on an old kitchen towel. Choose the threads you are planning to use carefully, picking out, perhaps, the colour of a favourite jug, the rich browns of wood surfaces or even the leaf colour of a pot plant. Cut out a template of the chosen shape in thin card. It is often an advantage to have different sizes of the same shape, so prepare as many templates as you will need. Arrange these along the border area of the towel, moving them around until you are happy with the arrangement. Holding the template firmly in position, dot round the edge with a water- or air-soluble marker pen on to the towel. (It is not possible to 'draw' round the template on towelling as this just ruffles the pile and the line disappears.)

Place the first part of the design in a metal ring frame. If this is near the side or bottom edge of the

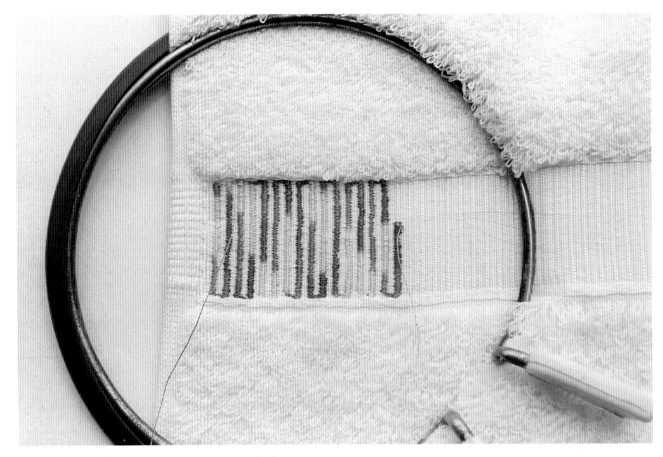

Border patterns suitable for embroidery on towels.

towel, this edge can be placed across the centre of the ring frame and will still be held firmly. Take time to ensure that the towel is really secure in the frame. When embroidering on new, fluffy towels, the inner ring has a nasty habit of springing out, just when you are not expecting it!

Set your machine for free running stitch with the darning foot in place. Stitch round and round the outline of the marked shape until the pile is flattened and the line is as thick as you want it to be. Move the frame along to the next area of the pattern and continue embroidering right across the towel. As well as working outline shapes, try filling some of the shapes with solid embroidery. It takes a little longer, of course, but adds dimension to the pattern.

Some machines have a horseshoe-type darning foot which is open at the front. These are excellent for use on smooth fabrics, making it easier to see where you are stitching. Do not use a horseshoe foot

Embroidered border pattern in progress on towel, showing method of framing the towel to commence the stitching. Narrow satin stitch using a shaded thread.

when embroidering on towels, however, as the open ends of the foot slip into the loops on the surface of the towelling fabric, bringing your stitching to an abrupt halt!

Many towels have flattened areas of pile as a border, or ribbon-type inserts. Look carefully at these – they can often be embroidered using the weave already there as inspiration. In the illustration below, the border has a ribbed effect. Set your machine for satin stitch, the feed dog down and the darning foot in place. Frame the border area, working narrow lines of close satin stitch up and down, covering the ribs.

A shaded or variegated thread looks very attractive, making a colour pattern along the border. If you have to break off the thread for any reason, try to work out what part of the colour you need when restarting or the break will appear unpleasantly obvious.

Work out a similar design and colour scheme for embroidery on face-cloths and bath towels. Change the scale or intensity of the pattern according to the size of the towel. You will soon discover how easy and practical it is to embroider on towels. The back will look identical to the front, and they can obviously still be washed in the washing machine.

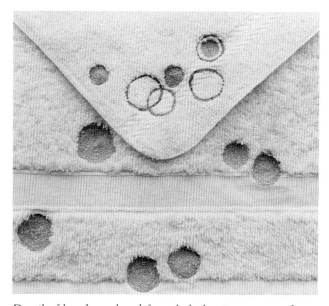

Detail of hand towel and face cloth showing pattern of circles in free running stitch.

Detail of hand towel showing border pattern of satin stitch, with face cloth worked in free running stitch, both using a shaded thread.

SHEETS AND PILLOW CASES

As with towels, add embroidery to your stock of bed linen. Even plain, old white sheets can look very special with an embroidered border picking out the colours in a bedroom. Purchasing embroidered bed linen can be very expensive and rarely co-ordinates exactly with your colour scheme.

Most sheets have a machined hem, so decide whether the embroidery will be contained on the hem, the area above the hem or across the join. Start with a simple satin-stitch border, worked with the machine set for ordinary sewing. Many people are wary of satin stitch, thinking that it looks hard and 'automatic', or worse, that it tends to pucker the fabric. Certainly, one line of satin stitch would be very ordinary, but massed, interwoven lines in varied colours or a shaded thread can look much more interesting. The method of stitching guarantees no puckers, the back is the same as the front and it does not take too long to work.

Mark where the border is to be with two parallel

Suggested patterns for borders on sheets and pillow cases.

Three border patterns worked on pillow cases. Top: free satin stitch. Left: lines of satin stitch just touching, with narrow line worked over the join. Right: satin stitch worked in the frame in various colours and stitch widths.

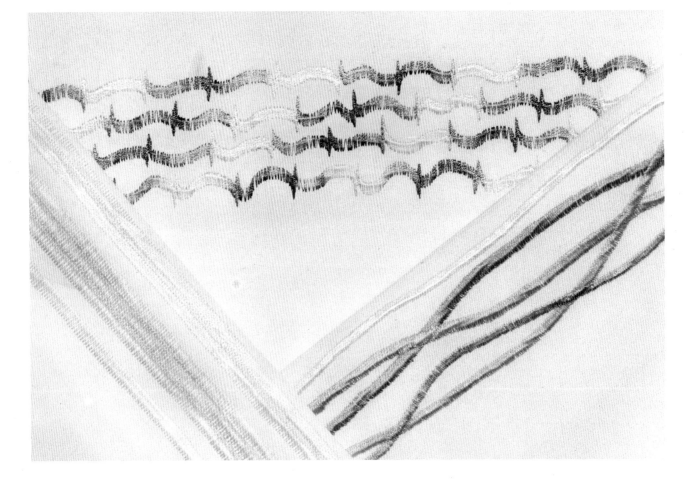

lines, say 5 cm to 7·5 cm (2 to 3 in.) apart, using a water- or air-soluble marker pen. It is essential to frame the sheet whilst stitching, even though you will be working with the feed dog up and the ordinary satin-stitch presser foot in place. This makes absolutely sure that the stitching will not pucker and also makes curved lines easy to control, without the need to pull at the fabric. It is also necessary to have a metal-spring ring frame as you will want to move the frame along the border without stopping stitching.

To start on the edge of the sheet, place it in the frame with the side edge across the middle. Set your stitch width to the maximum. Holding the frame firmly, you will find you can stitch in a curved, flowing line rather than just straight. When your stitching reaches the side of the frame, make sure the needle is down in the fabric before removing the inner ring of the frame. Slide the outer ring along, replace the inner ring and continue stitching right along the width of the sheet.

Work another line, perhaps with a slightly narrower stitch width and a different colour. Let the lines meander within the marked border area, crossing over each other. It is not necessary to mark each line to be stitched – only the extent of the overall border. Four or five lines of stitching can be worked within a 5 cm (2 in.) border.

A similar pattern of lines can be worked as free satin stitch. Use the darning foot, lower the feed dog and place the sheet in the frame as described earlier. The lines can now be much more flowing, worked in circular patterns using the full width of the border area. Add open areas of zigzag by moving the frame more quickly as you stitch, or broken lines by moving the frame sideways in parts. If you are nervous of your ability to stitch so freely, guidelines can be marked with a soluble pen.

Pillow cases can be embroidered to match the sheets with the same, or smaller, version of the design. Be very careful not to accidentally catch the back of the pillow case in the stitching. Machine embroidery is very difficult to unpick!

DUVET COVERS
Any of the design ideas for towels or sheets can be used for embroidery on duvet covers. The only problem is the large amount of fabric involved, and

Designs to be worked on a separate strip of fabric in free running stitch, then applied as a border pattern to duvets.

that the embroidered areas are usually wanted at the top end, far away from the opening.

Clear a really large area around your machine, checking constantly that you are working on only one layer of fabric. Many duvets are made of a patterned fabric or have some sort of border pattern on them. This can often suggest the embroidery, stitching lines around motifs or areas of the design, or adding extra decoration to an existing border pattern using your own colours.

For a more elaborate or intricate design, it would be better to work on a separate strip of fabric, applying this to the duvet with lines of running stitch or satin stitch, when the embroidery is completed.

CUSHIONS

Many of the techniques described in previous chapters are suitable for embroidery on cushions, whether these are intended for the sitting-room, bedroom or elsewhere. Choose the technique carefully, bearing in mind whether the cushion will need to be hard-wearing and washed frequently, or seen purely as a decorative furnishing accessory.

Whatever the purpose and technique, it is often the finishing touches which make the difference between an ordinary cushion and a really special one. Always consider the cushion as a whole when planning the embroidery, giving equal care to the choice of piping, cord or frill.

PIPING

Detailed instructions for inserting a piped cord on the edges of a cushion can be found in books devoted to soft-furnishing techniques. Usually this is a plain, bias strip of the same fabric, or perhaps in a contrasting colour. However, you can make the piping really decorative in its own right, complementing the embroidery used for the cushion.

Find the true bias line on the fabric, as shown. Mark a number of lines parallel to this line and to each other. The total length should equal that required to go round the cushion, plus seam allowances.

Stitch lines of embroidery on the straight grain of the fabric, going across all the marked, parallel lines. Work with the same threads and colours as used in the embroidery on the cushion. Try lines of satin stitch or zigzag, thin ribbons applied with straight

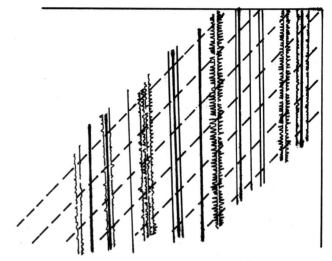

Cutting lines marked on the diagonal of the fabric, with rows of machine stitching worked on the straight grain.

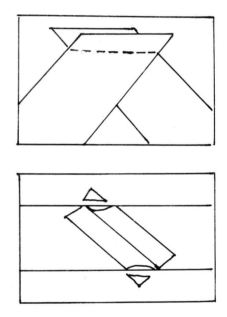

Method of joining short ends of strips of fabric to be used for piping.

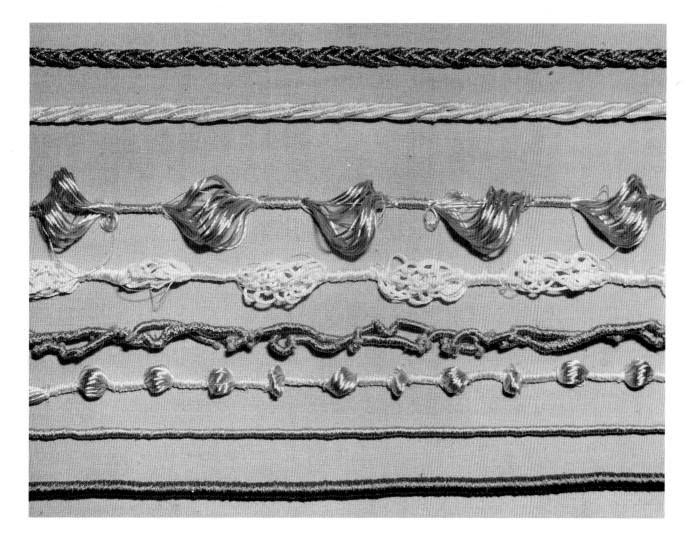

A variety of machine-wrapped cords, showing plain, twisted, plaited and gathered-up cords.

stitch or zigzag, lines of straight stitch in different colours or automatic patterns. On a cushion featuring twin-needle pin tucks, use this technique on the piping, or any appropriate combination of stitch patterns.

All these stitches can be worked with the ordinary presser foot and the feed dog up, as in normal sewing. It may still be desirable to frame the fabric, especially if it is very fine. When using a sheer or lightweight fabric, back this with muslin before adding the embroidery, to prevent the twist or texture of the piping cord showing through.

Cut the fabric into strips along the marked bias lines. It does not matter that you are cutting through

the embroidered lines – these will be secured when the piping is inserted. Join the short ends together, on the bias, forming a long strip as shown opposite. Proceed as for normal piping.

MACHINE-WRAPPED CORDS

It is surprising how few sewing-machine manuals mention this method. It is an essential technique for anyone interested in making soft furnishings or fashion accessories. The advantages are many. You can make cords of any thickness, twist or plait them together, vary the texture and, of course, they will exactly match the embroidered item they embellish. There are three ways to make the basic cord.

1 *With a braiding foot*
Most makes of machine will take a braiding foot, though this is not usually one of the standard

accessories. Ask your dealer if one is available for your machine. It is used to couch down braids and thin ribbons, but makes excellent cords too.

Choose a fine-string or firm-wool thread, checking that this will pass easily through the round hole in the braiding foot. Set your machine for medium-width satin stitch and the minimum stitch length. Thread the string through the hole in the foot, holding it and the two machine threads at the back of the machine. With your other hand, hold the string firmly at the front of the machine.

As you stitch, the needle goes from side to side over the string, completely encasing it with thread. Ease the string through evenly as you machine. Try to use string or wool close in colour to the machine thread you are using, just in case it shows through. The resulting cord is nicely stiffened and can be used alone or twisted with others to give a thicker braid.

2   With a darning foot

The disadvantage of using a braiding foot is that the thickness of the cord is limited to the size of the hole on the foot. For a slightly thicker cord, the darning foot can be used instead. Place the string under the darning foot, turning the fly wheel towards you by hand, to check the required width of the satin-stitch setting. The needle should just clear the string at both sides.

Remember to hold the string firmly at the back and front of the machine as you ease it through under the stitching. A little practice soon shows the best way to hold it: up at the back and pressed down on to the bed of the machine at the front seems to work very well. This stops the string wandering from side to side. If the stitching is a little sparse in places, ease it back under the needle to fill in the gaps.

3   Without a darning foot

Many machine embroiderers do not use any foot for wrapping cords. This method also allows you to wrap really quite thick strings, piping cord, and so on.

Set your machine for the widest satin stitch, remembering to lower the presser-foot lever to engage the upper-tension system. Your machine will stitch happily over the cord, although, as with all methods of wrapping, there is no fabric under the needle. As a precaution, always hold the spool and bobbin threads when you first start to stitch. On some machines, these have a tendency to disappear down into the race, causing a nasty tangle of threads which will require picking out with a pair of tweezers.

As soon as you see how easy it is to wrap cords, variations become obvious. Stitch over two or three strands of soft embroidery cotton or crochet thread. Then pull one of the threads up, gathering or puckering the cord along its entire length. Use many strands of a fine or floss-type thread, and machine short lengths of satin stitch, leaving areas unstitched. When one strand is pulled up, a very decorative, looped edging braid is obtained. This would make an unusual edging for lampshades or cushions.

Curtain tie-back. The deep-pink frill is edged with satin stitch. Tassels are threaded on to a machine-wrapped cord which is couched by hand to the top of the frill.

FRILLS

A gathered or pleated frill makes the most attractive edging for cushions, bed covers or curtain tie-backs. Co-ordinate this by adding some embroidery on the frill to complement the decoration on the item.

Unless the fabric is very thick, it gives a much better effect if the frill is made of a double thickness of fabric, ensuring that the back is as attractive as the front. As an incidental bonus, it is also much easier to embroider a narrow strip if it comprises two layers of fabric.

Cut a strip of the required length on the straight grain of the fabric. Join if necessary. Make it twice the width required for the frill, plus seam allowances. Fold the strip in half, ironing to form the crease. Whatever the chosen method of embroidery – whether ordinary stitching such as satin-stitched edge, or free embroidery – always put the frill strip across the middle of a metal-spring ring frame. This ensures that the stitching does not pucker the fabric, as well as giving maximum control. It will become second nature to slip the frame along the length of the frill whilst stitching. The professional finish you achieve makes the small, extra effort well worthwhile.

Folded strip of silk showing the method of working for a frill to be attached to a cushion. Free running stitch, worked at right angles to the folded edge, using two threads in the needle.

There are a number of embroidery methods suitable for frills, but the main consideration is to choose one which adds to, not rivals, the main design elements. Work out the total length required for the frill (as a rough guide, a gathered frill needs twice the length of the item to which it is attached). Always join the two ends together before working the embroidery.

Satin stitch, worked over the fold, makes a very neat and attractive edge. Set your machine for ordinary sewing, having experimented with different stitch widths and stitch lengths beforehand. These will vary according to the fabric and type of thread used. Massed lines of satin stitch, curving and crossing, will give a much bolder effect. Lines of free running stitch can be more subtle; these can be worked parallel with the edge of the frill or at right angles to the edge.

Sometimes a double thickness of frill would be inappropriate. The cushion on page 46 featuring frayed and woven strips has a frill of a single layer of fabric, cut exactly on the straight grain. A line of an automatic pattern is machined a little way in from the edge, with the fabric frayed back to this stitched line. This gives a pretty, softly gathered frill, in keeping with the style of the cushion.

TASSELS

Tassels are usually regarded as something to be made by hand (or worse, bought), but here is a really simple way to make them on the machine. It is so easy, in fact, that you may be tempted to add them to everything you make! They can add the perfect finishing touch to many soft furnishings, such as lampshades, pelmets, curtain tie-backs and cushions. As with cords, you can use the same thread as that in the embroidery, giving a totally co-ordinated effect.

The thread you choose to make the tassel is very important. The shiny rayon machine-embroidery threads are ideal. It is advisable to make a practice tassel – to ascertain how thick and long it should be, and whether the thread is suitable – before embarking on a major project.

1 Cut a template from medium-weight card, as shown overleaf. The length of this determines the length of the tassel and can, therefore, be varied.

A single tassel, a larger tassel with hand-wrapped head in a shaded thread, and a group of tassels, all made of rayon machine-embroidery thread. They are attached to machine-wrapped cords.

A template of 13 cm (5 in.) will give a tassel just under half that measurement.

Cut out the central rectangle, shaded on the diagram. Mark a central line across the sides of the card, with two equally spaced lines above and below. This is the measurement which will be machine-wrapped to form the head or loop of the tassel. For a small, single tassel 2·5 cm (1 in.) is ideal, but increase this for a larger tassel or when making a multiple group.

2 Catch the end of a reel of thread into the slit on one end of the card. Wrap the thread round and round, keeping it over the central cut-out rectangle. Seventy or eighty times is about right for a fine thread; less for a thicker one. Do keep a note of how many times you wind. Catch the end into the slit again, and cut off the thread.

3 Set your machine for free satin stitch, with the feed dog down and a medium or wide stitch width. You may choose to use a darning foot or not – whichever you prefer.

4 Place the wrapped card template in the machine, lining up your needle with the mark drawn on the side of the card. Do not forget to lower the presser-foot lever. Stitch over the central bundle of threads. In practice, it is best to stitch down one side, catching in the threads, to the mark drawn lower on the card, back up the other side to the top, then finally down the middle again. Make this last line of stitching as neat and even as possible. This gives a good firm wrapped effect for the head of the tassel. Leave long ends from your spool and bobbin threads.

5 Using sharp scissors, cut through the threads at the top and bottom of the card template to release the tassel.

6 Tie off the spool and bobbin threads (but do not cut the threads off yet).

7 Bend the wrapped portion over into a circle shape. Using the spool and bobbin threads, wrap the two sides together by wrapping one pair of threads in one direction and the second pair in the other direction. Tie off tightly. For a really secure finish, put each pair of threads into a needle and work up through the wrapped portion before cutting off.

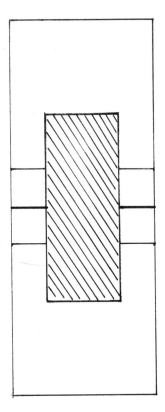

Template for a tassel, showing the slit at the top, the shaded area to be cut out and the drawn lines which determine the extent of the satin-stitch wrapping.

Stage-by-stage construction of a tassel, showing one finished tassel and a group of five tassels. For the latter, one tassel was made with a larger-size wrapped head, with four threaded through, attached by a machine-wrapped cord.

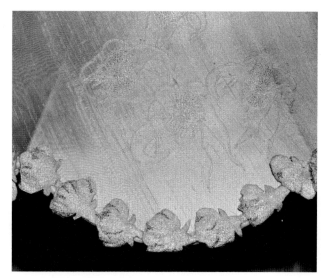

Painted-silk lampshade with design of roses worked in free running stitch. The rose petals on the edging were each worked individually using very dense free running stitch on a felt base, the density of the stitching giving the distorted, curling shapes of the petals (Annette Monks).

Detail of the lampshade.

Tassels can be threaded on to machine-wrapped cords to be attached in a variety of ways. Multiple tassels are made by putting a half-made tassel (between numbers 6 and 7 above) through one already finished. Then finish off the second one. The permutations are almost endless.

I hope that the illustrations in this chapter will inspire you to embroider articles for your home, whether large or small, subtle or spectacular. The knowledge that you have the skill to machine embroider, combined with making something beautiful and practical, is very satisfying.

Lampshade with fabric printing and a design of bats worked in free running stitch (Annette Monks).

5

EMBROIDERY FOR FASHION

EMBROIDERY on clothing conjures up many images. It may be the sumptuous court dress of Elizabethan times, the meticulous whitework of the Victorian era, beaded dresses of the 1930s, ethnic peasant embroidery or the high-fashion embroidery so popular today with the world's best designers. Over the centuries, it would be impossible to guess how many hours have been spent on the adornment of the clothes we wear.

This urge to embellish still remains, but we seem to be in instant, expendable times – here today and gone tomorrow – hardly compatible with painstaking hours spent on hand embroidery, when we know that the fashion may well have changed by next year. Machine embroiderers rarely claim that their craft is quick, but it is certainly quicker than hand embroidery. But, more than that, machine techniques can be rich or subtle, are hard-wearing and washable and have that all-important professional look.

As well as fashion itself changing, fashions in embroidery evolve with the times. It would not seem right today, for instance, to embroider a motif on a collar or pocket, or a border design round the bottom of a summer skirt. Instead, use the techniques described and the garments and accessories illustrated as inspiration for your own particular style and personal preferences in keeping with the mood of today.

GARMENTS

Although one embroidered pocket would seem dated by today's standards, lots and lots of embroidered pockets would be great fun as a decorative feature. Vary the size, overlap them or place many little pockets massed together on one large pocket.

Apply the same principle to cuffs on a shirt or jacket. Layers of overlapping embroidered cuffs, from wrist to elbow, would transform an otherwise plain shirt into a high-fashion item in your wardrobe. The embroidery need not be elaborate or highly coloured. The subtle pattern of the close meandering vermicelli stitch, described on page 36, makes a very effective texture. Use the same-coloured thread as the fabric, with just the glint of

.Blouse, tie, trousers and braces, made in various weights of silk fabric. The tie is marbled in soft shades of pink and green. The top of the trousers and the braces are richly embroidered with pin tucking, couched threads, applied frayed strips of organza, Italian quilting and applied, ruched and space-dyed ribbon yarn. The buttons are hand-painted (Linda Cook). Worn by Rachael Taylor.

Dress and jacket in space-dyed silk fabric. The quilted jacket has areas of stitching worked on water-soluble fabric, applied with space-dyed chiffon, nets and textured threads. The buttons are covered with silk fabric and embroidery (Celia Litchfield-Dunn). Worn by Abi Taylor.

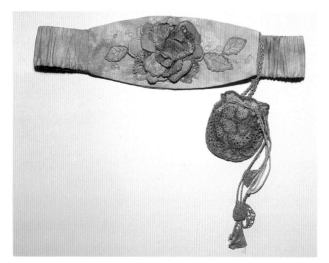

Space-dyed silk belt with applied rose. The petals are worked separately. Some are quilted with a satin-stitched edge, some are made of organza, some consist of stitching on water-soluble fabric, and some are of organza edged with stitching. The little bag is made of water-soluble fabric, and is attached to the belt with plaited, machine-wrapped cords (Celia Litchfield-Dunn).

Detail of a jacket. Layers of fabric quilted using running stitch, with areas cut back to reveal the different fabrics beneath (Della Barrow).

Quilted ski jacket. The fabric is space-dyed and stitched in a meandering pattern with lines of free running stitch. The collar, front band, pockets and sleeve seams are embroidered with lines of pin tucking which contrast with the quilted areas (Linda Cook). Worn by Abi Taylor.

Stitched slant pockets are repeated down to the hem (Linda Rakshit).

LEFT:
Christening shirt. Bands and an inserted frill of very fine vermicelli stitch using a gold metallic thread worked on cream-silk fabric.

the rayon thread highlighted on a matt surface fabric; or consider, perhaps, a shaded or metallic thread.

Machine-wrapped cords provide endless possibilities. They are flexible enough to be couched by hand or machine into the most intricate pattern, or used massed, side by side, to make a bold, textured band.

RIBBON YARN

This was originally introduced as a knitting yarn, and a close examination will reveal that it is a knitted tube, similar to French knitting. The rayon type has a silky appearance and dyes beautifully. Using a tapestry or blunt needle, thread soft wool through the tube, gathering it up to make a lovely textured yarn. Couch this, by hand or machine, between lines of pin tucking or satin stitch, for a rich decorative surface.

ABOVE:
Multi-cuffed suede jacket with punched and stitched eyelets (Linda Rakshit).

BELOW:
Detail of embroidery on the waistband of a pair of trousers, showing pin tucking, applied threads and strips of frayed fabric, Italian quilting and applied ruched ribbon yarn (Linda Cook).

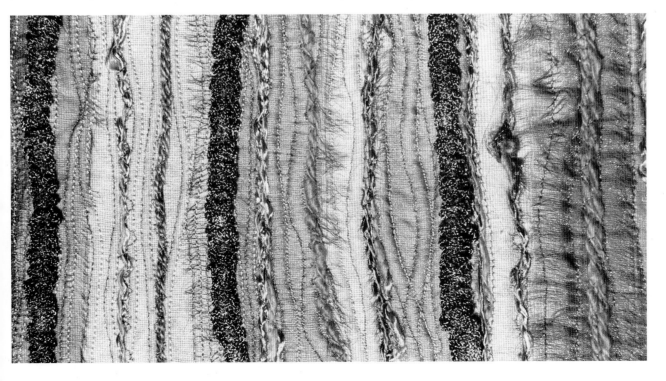

Bracelet of machine-wrapped elastic with attached pieces of solidly stitched felt. Ear-rings worked on a base of tights in a square pattern with the points curling over. Diamond-shaped ear-rings worked on a combination of wire and water-soluble fabric (Ear-rings by Frances Manz).

ACCESSORIES

Machine embroidery is the ideal technique for accessories, both for the delicacy of jewellery as well as the hard-wearing stiffness required for belts, bags and hats. The right accessory can add the finishing touch to any outfit, providing an element of fun, or the elegant focal point of an otherwise plain outfit.

RIGHT:
Neck piece and ear-rings. Stitching on felt, tights and water-soluble fabric, using dyeing and salt-resist techniques (Linda Cook). Worn by Abi Taylor.

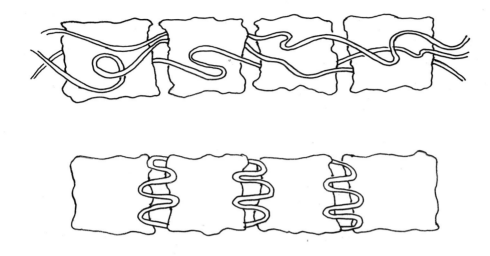

Two ways of joining solidly stitched pieces of embroidery for belts with machine-wrapped cords.

PELMET *VILENE*

This is usually found in the soft-furnishing department of large stores and provides the most useful base fabric for many accessories. It can be painted or dyed, used as the inner stiffener or as the base for machine stitching itself. Calico and pelmet *Vilene*, bonded together with *Vilene Bondaweb*, provides the ideal surface for dense, solid stitching, which can then be cut, distorted or moulded into any imaginable shape. It does not fray, and stitching can be worked right over the edges to provide little pieces of embroidery ideal for lacing together for belts.

Circles of sponge-painted pelmet Vilene, *overlapped and secured with free running stitch using a metallic thread. Some circles have a fringed edging worked over the pelmet* Vilene *on to water-soluble fabric. The bag is finished with machine-wrapped cords and embroidered circles (Della Barrow).*

The entire hat is constructed with shaped and moulded solid free running stitch with some pieces worked on water-soluble fabric and applied (Frances Manz).

WATER-SOLUBLE FABRICS

One of the most exciting embroidery developments of recent years has been the introduction of water-soluble fabric. You work free machine embroidery on this, but when it is immersed in water, the fabric completely dissolves leaving delicate, lace-like stitching. The fabric may not be available in your local needlecraft shop but can be obtained from specialist suppliers. Many advertise in embroidery magazines, offering a catalogue and mail-order service (see also the list of suppliers on page 95).

There are two kinds of soluble fabric. One resembles a fine organdie, dissolvable in hot or boiling water, and the other is a plastic (rather like a shower curtain) which dissolves in cold water. Many people prefer the hot-water variety as it feels and behaves as fabric and is, therefore, easier to stitch on, although it is more expensive. The cheaper cold-

Applied shapes using hand and machine appliqué. Additional decoration for the hat includes tassels and solidly stitched circles on machine-wrapped cords (Margaret Ross). See page 43 for detail.

water type tends to tear more easily, especially if the stitching is dense, but a patch of the fabric can always be added to cover a slit or hole. Sometimes, if working with children for example, dissolving in cold water may be preferable. Try both types if you can – you will soon discover which suits your purpose best. Whichever fabric you are using, proceed as follows.

1   Frame the fabric in a ring frame, setting your machine for free running stitch, with the feed dog lowered and using a darning foot if you wish. Both the top thread and the bobbin thread will be visible in the finished embroidery, so choose these with care.
2   Work several lines of free running stitch round the shapes. These could be simple flowers and leaves or abstract patterns of varying sizes of circles.

Whatever you choose, make quite sure that all the shapes are connected with stitching, or it will fall apart when the fabric is dissolved.
3   When completed, remove from the frame, cutting away the excess fabric from around the edges.
4   According to the type of fabric used, plunge into either boiling or cold water. The embroidery will shrink up alarmingly at this stage, with the fabric dissolving completely.

Detail of belt. Three-dimensional rose with some petals quilted and edged with satin stitch, others worked on water-soluble fabric and organza (Celia Litchfield-Dunn).

5 Rinse in cold water, stretch and pin to shape, and leave to dry. The lace-like embroidery may be a little stiff, which can, of course, be an advantage for some items. This is particularly so if metal threads have been used for the stitching.

6 If a softer finish is required, re-immerse in either the hot or cold water. Do this as many times as seems necessary. If a flat, smooth finish is required, the embroidery can be ironed. A combined fabric-and-lace effect can be achieved by pinning small pieces of sheer fabric on to the soluble fabric before stitching. Work over the edges of these on to the soluble fabric. After the immersion in water, the sheer fabrics are held by the lacy stitching between them.

Whether you use the hot or cold soluble fabric, the resulting embroidery is beautiful, with so many uses. Think of using it for appliqué, or as a narrow band inserted into the seam of a garment; for precious little bags, jewellery, hat decoration, lingerie – the list is endless.

Small bag attached to a belt. Worked on water-soluble fabric with machine-wrapped cords (Celia Litchfield-Dunn).

Necklace, ear-rings and a ring worked in free running stitch, combining shaped wire and water-soluble fabric (Frances Manz).

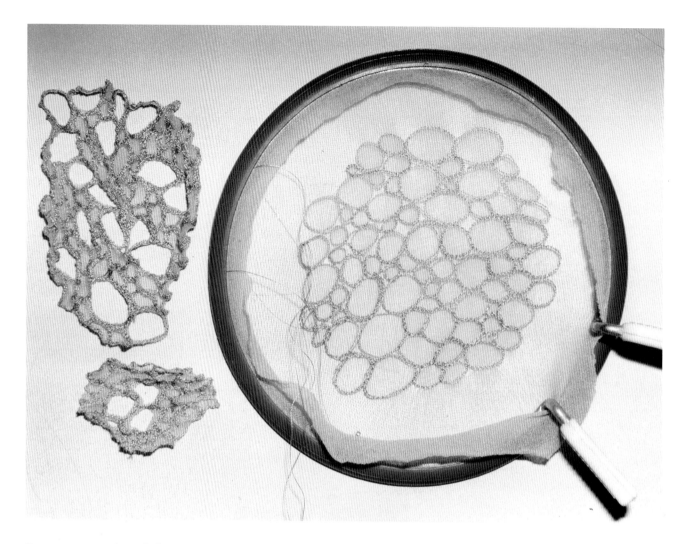

Free running stitch worked in circular patterns on tights in the frame. The detached pieces show the same embroidery with the excess tights cut away and the central holes cut out.

LACY EFFECTS ON TIGHTS

If you have difficulty in finding water-soluble fabrics, you may care to try this alternative. It is slightly denser, but still produces a lace-like open effect. It is embroidered on tights or stockings, the instructions for which are given on page 29.

1   Begin with fairly light-coloured tights, though you can always soak darker shades in a weak solution of household bleach. The colour of the tights will be visible in the finished embroidery. Rinse thoroughly when they have reached the desired colour.

2   Stretch the tights in a ring frame until the surface is as taut as possible. Work free running stitch in a series of circle shapes of different sizes. It is not essential to join or link all the shapes, as with soluble fabrics.

3   While the embroidery is still in the frame, cut out the centres of all the largest circles.

4   Remove from the frame, cutting away the excess tights from around the embroidery. The surface will crinkle up, looking quite delicate, but it is actually fairly strong, as is all embroidery worked on tights.

EYELETS

Many modern sewing machines have eyelet plates enabling you to work *broderie anglais* embroidery. Look in your manual index (probably listed under *English embroidery*) to see if they are available, or ask your machine dealer.

Use a fine thread and a closely woven fabric. It is a help to frame the fabric, enabling even, smooth stitching around the central hole. Practise using different stitch widths on satin-stitch setting and stitching round closely or with just a few stitches for a spiky-star eyelet. Do not cut the thread between eyelets, or the stitching will unravel.

Try using organdie or organza for a delicate effect which would look wonderful on lingerie. Always group eyelets together for maximum impact, perhaps using a shaded or variegated thread.

A larger-scale version of *broderie anglais* becomes cut work. Stitch several lines of free running stitch around the shape, cutting out the fabric from the centre with sharp, pointed scissors.

SPACE DYEING

Some of the garments and accessories illustrated have been made of fabrics previously space-dyed. This is a method of dyeing which produces marvellous mottled and merging colour patterns on fabrics and threads. It is easy to do at home in your own kitchen, and requires no special equipment. The method is suitable for silk, rayon and cotton fabrics.

1   Prepare all fabrics and threads by washing in hot soapy water and rinsing well. Calico should be boiled to remove all the dressing.
2   Tie thick threads into loose hanks and wrap thinner threads around a plastic ruler or length of plastic piping. The fabrics and threads should be damp. You will need a washing-up bowl or cat-litter tray and some cold-water dyes. Make sure that the dyes are for use with cold water, and not the hot-water washing-machine variety.

Detail of teddy (see overleaf) showing free running stitch, eyelets and cut work (Barbara Amos).

Teddy worked on organza with intricate areas of eyelets and cutwork (Barbara Amos).

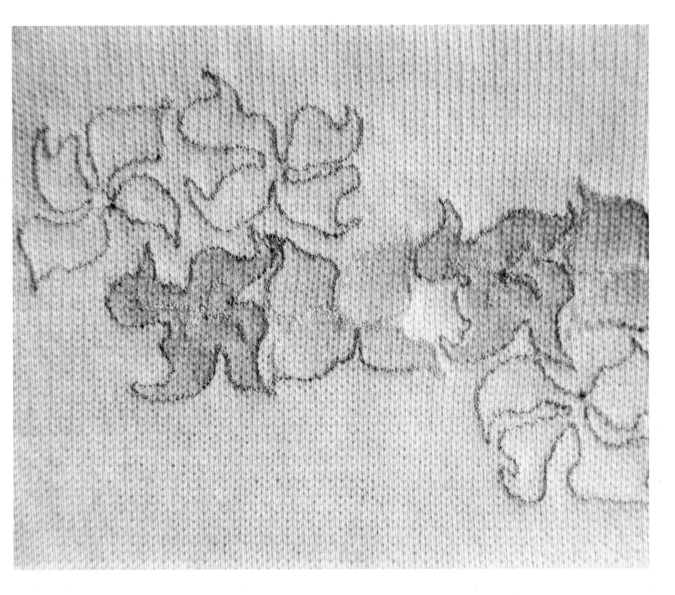

Printing on knitting outlined with free running stitch (see overleaf for technique).

3 Choose three colours which contrast strongly – red, yellow and blue, for example. This may seem a rather drastic colour scheme but will result in soft green, orange and lilac too.

4 Put a small quantity of one colour in a jam jar – about a mustard-spoonful – mixing with cold water to dissolve the dye powder. Do the same with the other two colours, each in their own jam jar. Fill all three jars about half-full with hot water, adding a teaspoon of household salt to each jar.

5 Place the fabrics and threads in the bowl, loosely arranged. For your first experiment, try small pieces of different fabrics such as silk, rayon and fine cottons, avoiding synthetic fabrics as these will not take the dye at all.

6 Spoon one colour of dye on to the fabrics, then the second and third colours in turn. Resist the temptation to fiddle, as handling the wet fabrics in the bowl will result in very murky colours. Left alone, the colours will merge beautifully.

7 Leave for about fifteen minutes. Mix one table-spoon of washing soda with 282 ml (half a pint) of boiling water and stir until dissolved. Pour over the fabrics. Leave for a further thirty minutes.

8 Pour the dye away, rinsing the fabrics until the water runs clear. Wash in soapy water and rinse again.

Variations in quantities, timing and colours used will always produce interesting results. Keep a record of such experiments with sample pieces. With a little experience, larger pieces of fabric can be dyed for garments and accessories.

KNITTED FABRICS

You may consider adding embroidery to a knitted garment or jersey-type fabric. The problem is obvious – you cannot stretch it satisfactorily in a ring frame to do the embroidery. If you attempted to do so, when the frame was removed and the tension released, the stitching would be puckered.

If you look at the back of a bought, embroidered jumper, you will probably see white fragments around the edges of the embroidery. This is the fabric stabilizer called *Stitch 'n' Tear*, which resembles paper. It is placed behind the area to be embroidered and torn away afterwards.

Cut a piece larger than the design, tacking it carefully behind the area to be worked. The fabric will then be stiff enough to hold, while you embroider using the darning foot. You may need to work two or three lines of free running stitch for it to show, as the stitches tend to sink into the surface.

Alternatively, work a line of very narrow-width satin stitch around your design. Very heavy, dense stitching on knitting can distort the feel and drape of the garment when worn. With this in mind, consider carefully where the embroidery is to be placed.

PROBLEM SOLVING

AGITATION can be the cause of many of the problems in machine embroidery – or rather in machine embroiderers. This is unnecessary if you remember that the vast majority of problems have both a simple cause and a simple remedy. Every time you identify and rectify a fault, you will be learning more about how your machine works, so try to regard problems as a positive learning tool.

The importance of a clean, oiled machine cannot be stressed too strongly. A neglected machine will continue, seemingly for ever, to stitch a straight line of ordinary sewing and this fact breeds a certain complacency in the owner. So the first golden rule is to clean and oil your machine at very regular intervals. The following is a guide to some of the more common problems.

TOP THREAD BREAKING OR SHREDDING

Learn more about the threads you are using. Break a short length between your fingers. Does it break easily? More easily than other threads? If so, reducing your top tension is the common-sense action to take. As a general rule, the more easily the thread breaks, the more you should reduce your top tension.

A larger-size needle should stop the shredding of the thread which occurs just above the needle. The use of a darning foot will also help.

BOBBIN THREAD BREAKING

This happens less often. The most likely cause is a tiny piece of loose thread caught in the race. Never wind one colour on top of another as this causes a tangle and, eventually, a breakage.

MISSED STITCHES

The use of the darning foot should help here by keeping the fabric in close contact with the base of the machine: the loop-stitch action of a sewing machine cannot function if the fabric is waving about in mid-air.

Tighten the fabric in the frame, and use a new needle, checking that the machine is correctly threaded.

INEXPLICABLE LOOPS

You have probably left the presser-foot lever up, so that you are stitching with no tension at all on the top thread.

Whatever happens, try not to get flustered. If your top thread breaks, find out why, rather than just 'trying a different one'. Do not fiddle with the tensions in the vague hope that all your problems will be solved. You must always know what you are trying to achieve by an alteration. Then – when the fault is cured – you will know why. As your ability and confidence grow with experience, problems really will become a rarity.

FURTHER READING

Embroidery magazine, published quarterly by The Embroiderers' Guild, Apartment 41, Hampton Court Palace, East Molesey, Surrey KT8 9AU

Landscape in Embroidery, Verina Warren, Batsford, 1990

Machine Embroidery, Gail Harker, Merehurst, 1990

Machine Embroidery: Lace and See-Through Techniques, Moyra McNeill, Batsford, 1985

Machine Embroidery: Stitch Techniques, Valerie Campbell-Harding and Pamela Watts, Batsford, 1989

The Art of the Needle, Jan Beaney, Century Hutchinson, 1988

SUPPLIERS

Barnyarns
Old Pitts Farm
Langrish
Petersfield
Hampshire

Borovicks
16 Berwick Street
London W1V 4HP

MacCulloch and Wallis
25–26 Dering Street
London W1R 0BH

Needle and Thread
80 High Street
Horsell
Woking
Surrey

Redburn Crafts
Squires Garden Centre
Halliford Road
Upper Halliford
Shepperton
Middlesex

Shades at Mace and Nairn
89 Crane Street
Salisbury
Wiltshire

Silken Strands
33 Linksway
Gatley
Cheadle
Cheshire

Whaleys (Bradford) Ltd
Harris Court
Great Horton
Bradford
West Yorkshire

INDEX